How to Achieve Total Prosperity

How to Achieve Total Prosperity

Mark Victor Hansen Ph.D. C.S.P.

1st Printing, 1981
2nd Printing, 1985

Published by
Mark Victor Hansen and Associates
P.O. Box 7665
Newport Beach, CA 92658-7665
Printed in United States of America

Contents

Special Thanks

Special thanks to my loving wife, Patty, who helped envision this to where it is, in your hands, and in the hand of millions more, and to Wanda Pate, my executive assistant, who untiringly shared the burdens of accuracy and gave suggestions which made it a much better book. I am immensely thankful for the expert editorial assistance given by John Zahody.

About the Author

He is a *MOTIVATOR*, not only in his speeches, his books, his films and tapes, but in his daily life. He is called "The Million Dollar Motivator" because he has inspired literally hundreds of life insurance agents to sell a single million-dollar policy by his dynamic seminars.

He is a *TEACHER* who finds as much joy in other people's success as he does his own. He has talked to over 500,000 people.

He is a *BUSINESSMAN*, who is President of three corporations and consultant to many more.

He is a *LEARNED MAN*, who was educated at Southern Illinois University, where he did graduate work with Dr. R. Buckminster Fuller. Mark now has his Doctorate in Mind Science from Golden State University, where he remains active as an Academic Field Advisor.

He is the *AUTHOR* or co-author:
Future Diary
Build a Better You—Starting Now
Stand Up Speak Out and Win
Joy of Selling

Foreword

Dr. Mark Victor Hansen presents the greatest eternal truths of God in a very practical way. He is illumined and inspired, and his writings go forth to heal, bless, inspire, elevate, and dignify the minds and hearts of all who cherish the eternal verities.

The Bible says, "I pray that thou mayest prosper and be in health, even as thy soul prospers."
Dr. Joseph Murphy
Laguna Hills, California

Prosperity is a thriving
state of economic,
family, social,
spiritual and mental
well beingness.

This book is dedicated
to you in the belief
that you can have
prosperity.

Introduction

Material Prosperity means that you have more than enough money to pay all your bills, invest in something that makes more money for you, and still have plenty of money left over to:
Do what you want to do,
go where you want to go,
buy *anything* you want to buy—
enjoy unlimited riches.
Prosperity is more than a material experience. It is having close and trusting relationships with friends. It is having the kind of people in your life with whom you enjoy sharing your experiences. It means having a successful family life and living together in harmony with those people whom you love and who love you. It means having a healthy body that is strong, full of energy and vibrant with peace of mind that allows you to sleep well at night.

It means keeping an open, active mind—a mind that is learning and expanding every minute of every day. It means that all the good things you do come back to you multiplied: Your life is overflowing with joy, friends, love, laughter, success, health *and MONEY!*

Chapter One
Twelve Principles of Prosperity

Twelve Principles of Prosperity

1. I think prosperous thoughts and I AM becoming ever more prosperous; thinking poor will make me poor.
2. My thoughts of prosperity always precede my demonstration and manifestation of prosperity.
3. My prosperity makes everyone better off, and no one worse off.
4. All prosperity starts within my mind. What I think about, comes about. The original source of all prosperity is God; and God can do no more for me than he can do through me.
5. My setting prosperity goals is a necessary prelude to getting prosperous. My first goal is to set goals that are definite, positive, specific, believable and attainable.
6. I'll "find a need/'want' and fill it." *Bernard Baruch*
7. My enjoyment of prosperity increases my prosperity.
8. I see, feel, believe, and take action toward my evolving prosperity.
9. I think big and I achieve big results. Money is

created in four ways: 1) I work. 2) Others work (management). 3) Money works (investment). 4) Ideas work.

10. To increase my prosperity consciousness I will increase someone else's. I teach what I most need to learn and it returns to me omnidirectionally.

11. My gift of giving is receiving. (I reap what I sow.) I sow generously, creatively, boldly, with an attitude of gratitude; my gift returns to me multiplied.

12. I have to do my own prosperity doing; no one else can do it for me.

Principle Number One:

I think prosperous thoughts and I am becoming ever more prosperous. (Thinking poor will make me poor.)

Prosperity is a state of mind. You've got to think right before you can do right and, thereby, receive unlimited prosperity. Most individuals would be astounded to know how many of their true beliefs are attached to thoughts of lack, limitation, shortage, and have-not-ness. Thoughts always reproduce themselves into life experiences. You are as prosperous or as poor as you are right now because your life demonstrates your historical and current beliefs about yourself. Change your beliefs and ultimately you'll change your experience. Individuals who think $10 thoughts get $10 results. But people like J. Paul Getty, Aristotle Onassis, Henry Ford, John D. Rockefeller, Andrew Carnegie and every other big wealth builder started small and grew fast. Each kept forever expanding his prosperity horizons for himself, his company, his family and staff. And by example, each inspired the world. Ultimately, each gained prosperity that evolved out of gargantuan services he conceived, believed in and delivered to the buying public. Whatever anyone else can do, you can do, if you want to fervently and completely enough. Your mind demands you to set the frequency dials on the amount of prosperity that you desire and deserve. The only limits are those that you self-impose.

In India, parents inadvertently pass on poverty from generation to generation, much like welfare victims who grow up on welfare and assume that they will always have to be on welfare. Therefore, poverty begets more impoverishment. What's truly impoverished is the individual self-concept—how he sees himself, affirms himself and feels about himself. The wonderful truth is that you can modify and rectify your self-concept by personal choice instantly and constantly, thereby creating a new and better you through which to express your full-humanness.

Principle Number Two:

My thoughts of prosperity always precede my demonstration and manifestation of prosperity.

"Judge not by appearances." What's visibly happening in the outside world may be of little importance compared to what thoughts an individual is thinking. In 1971, Mo Siegel was hired by people who paid him $1.50 per hour to be a walking billboard through the downtown streets of Boulder, Colorado. Not very prosperity-minded, you'd say, on external observation—but Mo was and is a great student of seeds and herbs. His body may temporarily have been a walking billboard, but his mind was creating a business to rival the gigantic Lipton Tea Company. Whenever Mo was not advertising, he was in the mountains collecting seeds for his Red Zinger tea and other special concoctions. He offered samples to friends, and eventually his deep thinking magnetized to him a businessman who became his associate, John Hay. Together they created Celestial Seasonings Tea Company, which, after only 10 years of business, is earning more than $10 million annually. Mo's powerfully desirous thoughts created and are continuing to create a growing business that is serving the taste and nutritional needs of a health-minded culture.

Your inner-knower knows how to make you as prosperous as you could ever want to be. Start where you are and aim high, while thinking and working yourself forever toward your goal. **Whatever you want wants you more than you want it.** The law of mind is that you can do as well as anyone else has done, is doing or will do if you use your mind as much as, or more than, he (or anyone else) has, is or will.

Principle Number Three:

My prosperity makes everyone better off and no one worse off.

Your prosperity can be omni-beneficial. In the Aquarian age of new thinking, we know we can create businesses in which everyone wins and no one loses. Employee-oriented corporations like Ed Land's Polaroid Company are evolving rapidly. World service businesses directed by totally conscious and responsible entrepreneurs now exist. You can prosper from the Golden Rule: "Do unto others as you'd have them do unto you," and its complement, "Do not do unto others (i.e. pollute, pillage, steal, corrupt) as you'd not want to be done unto."

Consciousness is an echo effect: whatever you put out, business-wise or otherwise, comes back; so smart folks are loving, prudent, thoughtful folks. With the advent of consumer education and inflation, individuals are increasingly purchasing what is best for themselves, i.e., more nutritious foods which are often less expensive (sugar- and preservative-free). As a result healthy buyers will be around to buy longer.

If one individual emerges from poverty, it is likely that his or her example will help hundreds, if not thousands, to do likewise. A great example is Dr. George Washington Carver. He evolved educationally and scientifically at a time when it was not easy for a black to advance. His creativeness with more than 300 peanut inventions, such as peanut butter, showed the whole world, and especially fellow blacks, that success was possible. Please read about him and visit the museum dedicated to him in Tuskegee, Alabama. It will inspire your creativeness.

Principle Number Four:
All prosperity starts within my mind. What I think about comes about. The original source of all prosperity is God; and God can do no more for me than through me.

Your mind is your source of unlimited, overflowing abundance. However, most individuals inaccurately believe that their good starts with someone else, someplace else, sometime other than now. The only time there is, is NOW. You can start your prosperity coming toward you by thinking about it. No other individual can give to you or take from you that which is yours alone to create via right of consciousness.

"In the beginning was the word"—or IDEA. You have only slightly less power to conceive whatever prosperous creation you'd like to, remembering always that the conceiver is greater than the concept.

While selling popcorn in front of a movie theatre, Kemmons Wilson, founder of the Holiday Inn, imagined himself being the "World's Greatest Innkeeper." Thanks to that great vision, we now get a new Holiday Inn room every 14 minutes. In addition, as conceivers, Kemmons and his partner, Wallace Johnson, have created tens of corporations emanating from the big ideas in their minds.

Little thoughts get little results; big thoughts get big results and, generally speaking, do more people infinitely more good. For example, Kemmons Wilson's idea, desire and action-oriented achievement exemplifies perfectly the *principle of cause, effect, and total resultant.* The *cause* was exclusively in the province of Wilson's mind. He could have said, "I am poor. I don't know anyone. Maybe it won't work. I am only a high-school graduate. No one will help me. I don't have the money. What if I fail?" and other negative, self-imposed propaganda that cancels any good, great, grand and terrific thinking. Instead, he purposely *affirmed* and *acted* on "I will *be* the World's Greatest Innkeeper." He took action. As Emerson said, "Every act is its own reward," and "Do the thing and you'll have the power." Kemmons did it. He built wholesome, affordable lodging places for family travelers. His idea caught on and he franchised it, exemplifying principle number three. Every franchisee was "better off," richer, thanks to Kemmons' idea. The *effect* was, and is, familiar places for people world-around to stay. The *total resultant* is an enterprise that is forever expanding, growing and improving: more places to stay, more employment, more money, a meeting center in almost every city and the creation of ever more products and services.

Principle Number Five:
    My setting prosperity goals is a necessary

prelude to getting prosperous. My first goal is to set goals that are definite, positive, specific, believable, desirable and attainable.

Isn't it curious that in a world of replete abundance, anyone ever experiences lack? The simple truth is that you can have virtually anything you *want*, tangible or intangible, if you'll *WRITE IT DOWN* and take the necessary sacrificing action to get it. However, it is factually true that less than 3% of humanity care enough about themselves to write down their true desires and get on with them. Yet the simple act of writing down your desires brings you to a point in consciousness where obtaining them is demonstrated already as a preview of future events, and all you do is proceed in right action to demonstrate that good. Individuals who write down their total desires are known to accomplish sum totally more than those who don't write down their goals. Cavett Roberts correctly says, "You can't get to a place you don't know about or get back from a place you've never been." So many folks want to arrive without making the trip.

Most people reading this need to set a *goal to set goals*. Do you? High achievers are forever reviewing, re-reviewing and adding to their goals. The beauty of achieving your goals is that you expand your horizons and can go on to new, higher goals.

Goals have to be *desirable, believable* and *specific* to facilitate your accomplishing them. Break down even your biggest goal into doable, daily parts. Too many individuals squander an entire life for too little because they neglected to plan extraordinary things to do. You are rare: you are reading how to do it. You've already distinguished yourself as ready to succeed. Now write down your every goal and compile that list in your future diary.

Every goal, no matter how big, is attainable, given time. Thanks to Werner von Braun and President John F. Kennedy we did the impossible, i.e., landed a man on the moon. Impossible means "I-m-m-m-that's-possible, given enough mind-power," or, "I-am-possible," because thoughts are things and everything is possible to the man or woman who believes. Your belief in the possibility of doing something or the impossibility of doing it predetermines whether or not you do it. Your belief controls your world. Be careful not to limit your visions to your current circumstances. Your concepts alone are the highways to your dreams and the realization of your loftiest desires.

Principle Number Six:

"I'll find a need and fill it," Bernard Baruch said.

Modify that slightly to "find a *want* and fill it." People do what they *want* to, not what they need to. When I lived and went to school in the Illinois Ozarks, I saw people living in shacks with outhouses. Almost everyone there owned a new or relatively new car and had a television antenna on his roof. Now, they may have *needed* indoor plumbing, especially a bathtub and shower, but they *wanted*, convinced themselves they could have, and ultimately purchased cars and television sets. Most of us do what our peer group does. My beloved mother always used to say. "Son, to be a great man, associate with great men and women." Likewise, association with prosperous people will encourage you to think, feel and believe in your ability to prosper. Conversely, associating with poor thinking will make you poor.

Every one of us has more talent than we use. And which of us, by suffering lack and self-imposed financial privation, can demonstrate his or her true talent? A parable says that if you bury your talent, you lose it. To under-finance the development of your great talent is to lose it, to the resulting detriment of yourself, your family and all who could benefit from it. Please, please write down your goals, as principle number five says. Manifest the talents you know you have and can polish up, make shiny and bright, so they reflect the light of who you truly are.

You have multi-million-dollar talents latent inside your mind, as stated in principle number four. These talents are begging you to get on a program to do all you can with them. God and the world needs, wants and desires every individual to totally, correctly and positively employ his or her full humanness.

Principle Number Seven:
My enjoyment of prosperity increases my prosperity.

You ought to enjoy totally whatever state of haveness you are experiencing, because your enjoyment of haveness will create more haveness to enjoy.

If you only have one dollar to invest in your experience, enjoy it. That dollar will encourage, excite and entice you to create more.

Enjoy paying your bills and it will become ever easier to pay them off and up, so that you can create new, bigger bills and know that the same process is true.

Many people suffering poverty-consciousness hoard their money, as Ebenezer Scrooge did. This financial constipation, in ultimate effect, creates have-not-ness. It also creates a money-rejection complex mentally, emotionally, socially and financially. People enjoy people who enjoy their relative and ever-expanding haveness.

Principle Number Eight:
I see, feel, believe and take action toward my evolving prosperity.

This can be scientifically stated as visualization, verbalization and imagination for or toward prosperity realization.

As Flip Wilson, in the "Spirit of Geraldine" says: "What you see is what you get!" Your mind is 87% controlled by your inner-visualization (seeing). Your self-image is the creative stuff of your mind. If you see yourself having only a little, that's what you'll achieve. See yourself having lots, loads, abundance and plenty and you shall have it. It's amazing what you can accomplish if you daily meditate in a mental state of controlled reverie and visualize the good you desire as yours already, then have a constructive attitude of gratitude as you thank, in advance of receiving that good, the source in you for giving it to you.

What you say is also what you get. Your inner-dialogue or verbalization controls 7% of your mind-power. So visualization plus verbalization affect and generate 94% of your life. This fact is too important to allow it to control you; you must discipline it.

Imagination is the workshop of the mind, wherein you create all that was, is, and ever will be. Most of our mental dials are tuned in on fears, doubts, indecision, pain, procrastination, guilt, anxiety, and other self-defeating, self-immobilizing behaviors which stifle and stop our prosperity. The subconscious cannot take a joke. If you imagine not being able to pay the bills, get a new car or whatever, you won't be able to do it. However, if you become a self-master and tell your thinking how to think and your feelings how to feel, controlling your imagination exclusively in the direction you want it to go, you'll realize every good thing you imagine and much, much more. You'll be standing under life's spout where all the good things of life pour out.

Principle Number Nine:

I think big and I achieve big results. Money is created in four ways: 1) I work. 2) Others work (management). 3) Money works (investment). 4) Ideas work.

The size of your thinking in each of these four categories determines, in advance, the size of your results.

1) "I work." You know how to work, but are you maximizing yourself? Are you rendering the highest quantity of the highest quality of service with a postive mental attitude, in order to obtain the highest possible rewards for services and contributions rendered? Most of us operate below our abilities and know inside this is true, which makes us feel guilty and less than we are. Instead, try constantly to out-serve yourself and watch the butterfly inside you break from his or her cocoon and gain high flight. Like the butterfly, your transformation will take on a form that you, now, cannot fully conceive of in beauty, elegance and completeness. Your love affair with work will make the transformation effortless effort.

2) "Others work" is the management principle of getting results through other people. When you're good you want to multiply yourself. Do so by associating with and creating what Napoleon Hill in his excellent book *Think and Grow Rich* calls a "Master Mind Alliance (MMA) Principle." In an MMA, you have two or more people working in a spirit of cooperative harmony to achieve one or

more definite major objectives. This creates a third new mind that is synergically more capable than an individual mind working alone. This incredible new ability creates a greater, bigger reality for all involved. When picking members for your MMA, get the best talent available: choose individuals better than yourself. Individuals with a low self-image generally choose people weaker than themselves and, ignorantly and inadvertently, sabotage their own greater good (see principle number eight on self-image).

3) "Money works." It's not enough to earn money—your money should be wisely invested so it can earn more money at a rate greater than the rise of inflation, while fully tax-sheltered. It's fun to study money in seminars, books, discussions and in your mind, and to experience and create successful, profitable investments.

There are only six kinds of investments:
- Banks and money instruments
- Insurance companies
- Real estate
- Gold/silver/diamonds/antiques
- (Small) businesses
- Stocks/mutual funds

Most people, never having reviewed such a list, assume that investment possibilities are infinite. What is infinite is the number of ways you can use these six vehicles.

4) "Ideas work." There is no limit on the value of an idea, except your thoughts, feelings and beliefs about it. Ideas employed create prosperity. This treatise was my idea, which is prospering us both. Create ideas for yourself.

When Dr. Russell Conwell was touring America giving his classical speech, "Acres of Diamonds"—a speech he delivered more than 4,000 times, earning more than $6 million with which he founded Temple University—he particularly inspired one woman. She heard Dr. Conwell say that everyone has great creative, inventive ideas that are worth vastly more than all the gold ever mined. She believed him in spite of her doubting husband. Later, in her job as a menial file clerk pinning collated papers together, she stuck herself with a straight pin and had an intuitive flash that there had to be a better way. She invented the paper clip and became a millionaire. Today, in the center of Philadelphia, a six-story-high paper clip stands as a constant reminder that anyone can have a life-serving, life-benefiting, life-prospering idea that will make everyone better off and no one worse off.

You too, are an inventor. Try to invent something that will prosper yourself and others.

Don Dible and I created the book series *Build a Better You—Starting Now*. Don had the idea for a multi-authored book series, the Encyclopedia of Motivation. Once he birthed the idea, it bloomed into 26 volumes with 365 different authors, one for every day of the year. This arrangement is a blessing to each writer, for he or she can create a chapter with relative ease and then merchandise it at his or her seminars. Readers get countless inspirational, educational and motivational benefits. Currently we estimate that this idea will sell more than 2.6 million copies, generate in excess of $26 million, and positively touch the lives of one-tenth of America's population.

Ideas work!

Principle Number Ten:
To increase my prosperity consciousness, I will increase someone else's. I teach what I most need to

learn and the results of my effort return to me from all directions.

We each teach what we most need to learn. I admit wanting to be very prosperous. I love the notion and experience. I feel no competition whatsoever. I want for you whatever you want for yourself. My desire is for everyone to be rich and lead a glorious and totally fulfilling life. There is enough good for everyone. Dr. R. Buckminster Fuller has shown by his life works that humanity has never had it, sum totally, so good. Life is better now than ever before. In 1900, 1% of humanity was physically and economically successful. Today 67% of humanity enjoys a standard of living better than that of the kings and queens of antiquity. Mass communication and transportation make us aware of the urban ghettos, India's poverty and Pakistan's problems—all of which are reversible when and if we choose to solve these problems.

It's true that we cannot make a weak person or a poor person either stronger or richer by making a strong or a rich person weak or poor. Instead, the constructive teaching of these principles, as herein outlined, is the vehicle that will release each individual's unlimited, overflowing prosperity, which will work to shower others with more prosperity.

Study and teach prosperity principles and they will bring you dividends and rewards that are unknown to common folks. The world will thank you in many ways for so teaching.

Principle Number Eleven:
My gift of giving is receiving. I reap what I sow. I sow generously, creatively, boldly, with an attitude of gratitude and it returns to me multiplied.

Bob Hope is a near-perfect example that "life gives to the giver and takes from the taker." His philanthropic activities are known everywhere, world-around. In his high seventies, he is a constant giver and receiver. The low-minded person says, "Rich people are crooks." Hope's generous outpouring of love and life has netted him the affection of humanity itself. His manager says, "Bob, if you had to live your life over, you wouldn't have time to do it." That's what Abe Maslow would call a "self-actualized life." You can do as much, if you would just get on with it. Hope's real estate holdings exceed one-half-billion dollars in value, and he currently receives $35,000 per 45-minute performance. Why? Because he continually outperforms, outserves and outgives himself. You can too, if you want to. Do you want to?

Principle Number Twelve: **I have to do my own prosperity doing—no one can do it for me.**
Likewise no one can eat for you; this is self-explanatory. I only recommend, as with all these principles, that you review them, mornings upon arising and evenings just before retiring, for 30 days until your mind owns them, understands them and uses them completely.

All these principles are stated in the first person, because all real learning is self-learning. Congratulations on your prosperous evolution.
HAPPY PROSPERITY!

Prosperity Afterword

Prosperity is an inside job. It starts inside your mind. You have a right to grow to any level of prosperity that you would like and love to achieve.

"Prosperity," Webster says, "is a thriving state of economic well-being." That's true. It is wonderful to have surplus. Money is something you need until you have enough to make you and yours comfortable. You need money until you feel you have it, conveniently to use as you choose. It is good to grow through financial satisfaction into financial independence with all the freedoms it offers. It is within your ability right now to create mentally that idea of prosperity. The idea comes from your self-generated *desire*. The true desire for prosperity will lead you to a *decision* to achieve prosperity. The desire and decision combined with *persistent discipline* will give you anything you want.

Real prosperity is more than money. It is a state of mind and a standard of living. To achieve total prosperity you will want to be financially, mentally, physically, emotionally, socially and spiritually well-off. You can have total prosperity, as outlined herein, that is omni-beneficial to you, your family, your friends, your business, your clients, and the world. Achievement happens through the continuing use of your positively evolving personality, services, and products.

Walt Disney is an example of an individual who achieved total prosperity. An American original, he developed animated films and created Disneyland and Disney World for all to enjoy—forever. He was universally loved, respected and admired. Disney prospered everyone with his rich consciousness, and everyone in turn has prospered him and the organizations which outlives him. Again, real prosperity is a state of mind. Walt Disney created a consciousness of an imagineer. He intuitively knew the law of mind. If you can imagine something, believe in something and feel it as real, you can create it.

Your mind, like Walt's, may really need, want and desire a gigantic project like Disneyland to manifest your full talents. Fearlessly dare to use these twelve prosperity principles. They work when you work them.

To one individual, prosperity is having one car, one home, and enough to sustain himself and his family. To another, the Hearst Castle is just a beginning. Your thoughts create your world. We all get rich, wealthy and prosperous to the degree that we truly want to. How much do you really want? Look at what you have currently and you will see what you have truly wanted up until now.

Prosperity is! It's ready for you whenever you are ready for it. One of the world's most prosperous women told me that she had owned oil rights for over 25 years. One day she decided she wanted to move herself from being wealthy (comfortable) to being rich (able to afford anything she wanted). Incidentally, she is a totally self-made millionaire who, I hope, will soon write her inspiring story. She told me that to feel rich, she meditated energy into her feeling experience for one and one-half hours. She was suddenly overcome with excitement and felt, "God, I've got it made!" Three days later her business associate called and encouraged her to drill the "Dakota" well 7,700 feet deeper for more oil. For more than 25 years this could have been done. The oil had been there all the time, but she had had no awareness or consciousness to generate its coming up. Besides, 25 years earlier, the price of crude was $4.65; now it is $32.50. The price of gas was 12½¢; now it is $1.30. The prosperity came in at the extent of her imagination, as it does with yours.

When you set prosperity goals, it is good to have a base, i.e., "I'll not earn less than $10.00 an hour and I'll put no lid on it." You are worthy to be prosperous because you are alive.

The prosperity in you needs you to create a

reason to bring it out. See yourself now realizing your full prosperity potential.

Chapter Two
Prosperity Thinking

Chapter Two
Prosperity Thinking

Prosperity is a thriving state of well-being in a total sense, physically, mentally, spiritually, socially, familially and especially financially. It provides you the freedom to do what you want to do, when you want to, because you want to do it.

Prosperity thinking eventually fosters the truthful understanding that all wealth of the universe is at your command to control, accumulate and *use*. You can ultimately satisfy your every want, need and desire.

To prosper greatly, you must be a pro, a real professional—a professional thinker who knows how to control his or her thinking to ingest, digest and egress exclusively prosperity thoughts. The law of mind is that what you think about, comes about. A mind moored to right prosperous thinking and right prosperous action guarantees right prosperous results—RIGHT HERE AND RIGHT NOW.

Every individual has the greatest power of all, the power to choose how he or she is going to think, act and react to situations, circumstances and people. We create our own destinies in our minds. It's in our minds that we must be disciplined to dwell exclusively on expanding our and everyone else's prosperity.

Prosperity is the most easily and effortlessly

acquired asset of a mind focused thoughtfully and studiously on it as a subject area. Life wants you to live fully and abundantly with avalanching and overflowing good coming your way.

You must start with the general idea: "I am rich." This is because the mind is deductive and works from general to specific, proceeding to create the truth, thought and fulfillment that you are rich. Therefore act in ways that will facilitate the ever greater creation of more prosperity.

Prosperity is a win-win-win game. Everyone is better off when you prosper honestly and sincerely, using your consciousness to create ideas that will earn for you all that you could ever want, need, or desire.

You have an unlimited financial potential, if you but start where you are and keep expanding your desires in believable and achievable steps. The more you do, the more you can do. Feeling like a millionaire helps you to generate the ideas a millionaire would have. You visualize money pouring in, and this evokes in you a euphoric feeling. Wealth is your new attitude. You have a growing awareness of wealth. You trust that your ideas, attitudes and capabilities will pay off someday soon. You visualize surplus, not merely survival. Survival does not excite your imagination except in times of distress.

One man told the author that a computer equal to a human mind would be worth $100 million. Therefore, YOU are worth $100,000,000.00 U.S. dollars. Your mind is omni-capable and you can and do choose to start thinking $1 million thoughts, and even $100 million thoughts, rather than thinking lack thoughts of only $1 or $10 or $100. Think bigger thoughts and you will get a bigger harvest.

Prosperity is a gift of God. Everyone is born

prosperous. Their minds are equipped at birth with more capacity (prosperity of brain-cells) than will ever be used. Today, the gifts of thousands of prosperity scholars are available to you in book, tape, and film form. All you need to do is read one, get the idea and work with it. It's easy and beneficial to everyone.

The world started prosperously, is now prosperous and will always be prosperous. It requires a certain kind of vision to see the extraordinary availability of whatever you're ready for. The world began with an inventory of every good thing in it, not with just sufficient supply for life-support but with an abundant and omni-regenerative supply.

Humans started in habitation of earth on the South Sea Islands (called the Carolinas). Born naked, helpless, and ignorant but possessing thirst, hunger and curiousity, they had available to them abundant vegetation, fruit and fish. Today, human mental energy applied appropriately and world-around has vastly more scientific ability to generate food, transport it and store it for use by 4 billion-plus inhabitants. We can feed everyone. As this idea becomes believable, it will be achieved. Humanity has never had as many individuals successful, thinking, and advantaged by such wide tool capability. The abundances available due to scientific and technological advances are small in comparison to what is about to happen as the human mind unfolds it's total capabilities.

Anyone can get prosperous almost instantly today if they but acknowledge and use the laws of prosperity and the population base of 4 billion inhabitants on our Eden called Spaceship Earth.

Prosperity
Ernest Homes said: "If you insist that poverty

and goodness come in the same capsule, I'd like to have you explain to me why a hungry man is more saintly than a well-fed man."

If some prosperity is good, what's wrong with a whole lot of prosperity? And even better yet, with prosperity that prospers everyone around you to their own greater good? If each one can teach one, eventually "every person could fish for him or herself" and be joyously prosperous. In such a utopian world, individuals would prosper with good self-esteem, possess positive and correct self-love, and the world would work for 100% of humanity because everyone would volitionally choose to make it work.

Obviously, if happiness is good, more happiness is better. Likewise if money is good and experience-wise stewardship of that money is being used for right action, then everyone is better off and no one is worse off.

Money is energy. Einstein taught us that energy is constant, 100% accountable experience that merely undergoes many transformations between mass (pent-up, congealed energy) and energy (radiant, moving energy). Likewise, money is created exclusively by consciousness and consciousness is the creator of money, in whatever form it takes—shells, beads, barter, coins, gold, paper, or computer-accounted balances. Unfortunately, most of humanity is unaware of the laws of mind (i.e., that "thinking makes it so...") or the laws of money (i.e., think abundance and you'll achieve abundance vs. think poverty and you'll experience poverty). So like mass which is stored energy, most individuals have potentially many millions of dollars pent up in their minds waiting and wanting to be discovered and used to their own greater good.

Your mind has an unlimited supply of money awaiting your creation. Dr. R. Buckminster Fuller has taught that real wealth (RW) equals energy (E) integrated with intellect (I): RW = E + I. Intellect is always learning more and using energy ever more profitably, thereby increasing real wealth.

Poverty is a degrading, dehumanizing, cancer-like disease of the uninformed mind. It makes thieves, robbers and murderers out of individuals who would be loving, if they'd been taught the truth that creating prosperity honestly is easy and omnibeneficial, offering deep feelings of self-love, joy and satisfaction that are profound and lasting. Lack of money has awful and insidious effects like driving people to drink or use drugs to escape their lack and misery temporarily. Others have used murder to get their inheritance early, and have suffered constantly as a result. Others have used arson or suicide to get an insurance policy to pay off their bills for their families or business associates. Crimes of all sorts are committed by people who are inspired to seek a thrilling, easy way to make a fast buck. What these folks misunderstand is that service is the only rent we pay for space we occupy. It feels good to serve, and right service always ends poverty, right now.

God does not limit us. Only we can limit ourselves with our own ignorance.

Please read and reread this book until you totally apprehend and comprehend the spirit of this vital message. Soon you will understand that abundance is the truth of the universe, a billion galaxies with a trillion stars each, and you are abundant with 18 billion brain cells begging to be put to work by a goal. You set the goal to be prosperous. Make the goal definite, positive and specific. Make it believable, desirable and obtainable. Take positive action and you shall have it. CONGRATULATIONS!!!

Prosperity is having as much as you want, need and desire, or being able to create as much as you need, when you need it, to do what you want to do. Likewise, a prosperity state of mind will never have you doing something you don't like for money or stop you from doing what you want to do because of lack of money. Rather your mind will always create surplus beyond expenses and be ready with ideas that can generate money immediately to meet any need. That's my definition of prosperity. It's good to have some surplus, but too much is excess, unless you're employing it to do the most good and least harm, as Andrew Carnegie tried to do.

(1) Our tendency is to look only to the immediate and try to live our future thoughts out of our present circumstances.

Realize that prosperity thought-forms implanted in your mind need encouragement, time to grow, and constant little reinforcement affirmations that promise you that you will be prosperous because of the actions you are now taking. DON'T QUIT! Start now in harboring, harvesting and acting on your prosperity ideals. Look forward to the next prosperous moment, hour, day, year, luncheon, or nice little visit to a prosperous place, like the Planting Fields Arboretum on Long Island in New York. Visiting the homes and museums of the very, very rich gives you the feeling of their presence, thoughts, ideas and personhood; it's a great inspiration. Then, meditate deeply on your ever more prosperous tomorrows, where you'll be spending the rest of your life creating similar retreats and sharing them with posterity.

(2) We shall never learn how to grow rich by

studying poverty. Rather, become a student of wealth, learn the law of opulence and become opulent.

The law of opulence is this: visualize, verbalize and feelingly believe in your progressive opulence and you shall have it.

Where your attention goes, your energy flows. Put your attention on poverty, lack and limitation and you will manifest the same because you are reinforcing those causal thoughts which result in that kind of experience, condition and circumstance.

Change your thinking (cause) and you will change your results (effect). If I could open up your scalp and read your thoughts, I could tell you the price tags and values that you have self-imposed and can self-accelerate, if you choose.

Mentally focus only on what you want to create in your present and future experience.

Prosperity's biggest plus is that you are thinking about it. Never before has the majority of humanity been privileged with so much re-investable time to think about prosperity, to consider how to make themselves and others evermore prosperous.

In the history of the evolution of prosperity, never have so many been willing to share what becomes obvious once you start seeing with an open, believing eye. The majority of humans are about to become prosperous in every good way. We have come to a critical-mass time where the many will come to know and believe that it is normal and natural to be rich. Shared wealth will abound and astound everyone. The Garden of Eden called Earth will bloom with living perfection. Why? Because progressively we're eradicating the fear of lack.

What is your self-imposed prosperity limitation?

So many look out the windows of their present circumstances and feel poor. Embrace the greater possibilities and bigger ideas, the things that Russell Conwell termed the *Acres of Diamonds* (read this classical book) within themselves. You alone determine your inner growth and can change the decimal point in your income, when you really want to. Your future earning power is an inside job— inside your mind. The beauty is that the mind seeking prosperity gets stronger and deeper in its pursuit. Your mind is inexhaustibly resourceful if your desire is sufficient. You choose to work beyond the ordinary eight-hour day and gain positive momentum to become extraordinary by investing extra time, effort, energy and money to obtain your dream.

Life does not choose a few individuals to prosper at the expense of the many. Each one of us can prosper to the degree that he or she will back visualization, verbalization and imagination with creative actions that result in successful demonstrations.

Prosperity has never been easier to achieve than it is right here and right now. Prosperity is available to those who consistently discipline their thoughts, words, actions and results.

In 1900, 1% of humanity was physically and economically successful. Today 67% are, according to Dr. R. Buckminster Fuller's World Resources Inventory at the University Science Center in Philadelphia, Pennsylvania (a place to visit). Things are good and they are going to get better, especially if you're creatively using your mind to make them better. If we make the right decision we get utopia, otherwise oblivion.

My prosperity does make everyone better off and no one worse off. Old lack-thinking erroneously assumed that if someone had more, someone else would have less. This concept springs from the amalgamation of Malthusian and Darwinian theories. Thomas Malthus, a British economist working in India in 1797, saw population increasing geometrically (2, 4, 6, 8) while food production increased only arithmetically (1, 2, 3, 4). With insights that the world was spherical, he assumed there was "not enough to go around." Charles Darwin, about that same time, posited his theory of "survival of the fittest." Add those two ideas and you get lack-thinking: "There is fundamental scarcity and only the strong survive, therefore it's either you or me—so goodbye to you."

The truth is that Malthus did not know about the simultaneous inventions of refrigeration—created out at sea—and hermetic sealing, plus other enhanced food preservation and growing techniques that made Malthus and Darwin wrong.

Today, more people are thinking and creating. Moment by moment we are having breakthroughs that benefit every one of us in all ways. Agriculturally, we have hydroponics, desalination, artificial insemination and many, many more breakthroughs that will prevent our systems from breaking down.

When an individual close to you prospers and exemplifies the law of prosperity, others start believing and acting like they can also. The individual acts as a vital, vibrant inspiration to others. Reverend Ike says: "My having 19 Rolls-Royces does not prevent you from deciding to have one, 19 or even more." He is not only teaching people how to fish for prosperity—he stands as an example. Believing in right thinking and right action, Reverend Ike started 10-plus years ago with nothing and now has had over $40 million circulate through his experience annually, creating ever more and stimulating others greatly to go out and do likewise.

The law of abundance is like the sunshine. It gives its radiance regularly, abundantly and non-judgmentally. It never says, "I don't like that tree, flower or person so I'll hold my light and warmth from them." Rather, consider the warm glow of the sun in an area that has a high incidence of radiation, like Boulder, Phoenix or San Diego. On a sunny day, as many can sit in the sun and healthfully tan themselves as choose to. The sun has no favorites. It would love to beautify your skin with a delightful tan. Your body rejoices when it gets to play joyfully in the warm outdoors, being kissed tan by the abundantly generous sun.

The law of abundance only knows how to give from its unlimited, infinite resource storehouse. As the Master said, "ask and ye shall receive."

Write down your own 10 reasons for becoming prosperous. The author's include:
To buy free time to be with
 1. myself
 2. my wife
 3. our children
 4. our businesses
 5. the church
 6. various philanthropies
and also
 7. to reward myself because I desire and deserve it
 8. to exercise my true talents
 9. to benefit total humanity
10. to make the world work

What are your 10 reasons? In goal-setting we know that the individuals who accomplish the most do so because they have what is called "stacked motivation," or a multiplicity of reasons why they want to succeed.

Poverty Message Imprinted From Parents

The inner-dialogue tapes that replay continuously in your subconscious came from early, important influences like your parents and significant others. They may be misprogramming you now at a rate of 1,200 words per minute, the speed at which your mind thinks. You see, 9 out of 10 inputs you receive are negative in nature, so you must personally choose to think positively and creatively, dispelling the negative always, at all times and in all places. You'll have to spend half your time editing and rescripting those program scripts.

Lines from negative scripts sound like this:

—"You think I am made of money."

—"A penny saved is a penny earned."

—"Who do you think I am, Rockefeller?"

—"You spend money like a drunken sailor."

—"In the Depression we learned the value of money."

—"Clean your plate, there are children starving in China."

—"You stingy _____." (or other profanities)

—"You're going to nickel-and-dime me to death."

—"Someday you'll just have to learn you can't have everything you want!"

—"Well, at least you got more than a penny for your tooth."

—"I am awful with money."

—"I can't even balance my checkbook."

—"My credit cards are always over limit."

—"I always write rubber checks."

Your waking mind actively inputs data 16 or so hours per day = 365 days per year = the number of years of your life. Knowing that, consider how much relative negation you must overcome with consistent, persistent affirmation and visualization. Enjoy the process, for you will love the end result. To rejuvenate your thought processes, write these prosperity proclamations on 3x5 index cards. Tape one of them to the dashboard of your car, your bathroom mirror or your desk. Read it feelingly. Try to live it. Once the message is truly felt, rotate to the next prosperity proclamation. These thoughts frequently and regularly repeated (cause) will inevitably find their way into your experience (effects).

Chapter Three
Prosperity Proclamations

Prosperity Proclamations

—MONEY IS FLOWING TO ME IN INCREASING ABUNDANCE.

—I DESIRE AND DESERVE MONEY AND WILL USE IT FOR MY GOOD AND THAT OF OTHERS.

—I AM A MULTI-MILLIONAIRE.

—CREATIVE MONEY-MAKING IDEAS IN ME ARE ATTRACTING MORE AND MORE *MONEY TO MY GOOD* USE(S).

—MY INNOVATIVE THINKING IS MAKING ME AND OTHERS VASTLY RICHER.

—THE MONEY I CIRCULATE GOES OUT DOING EVERY KIND OF GOOD AND RETURNS TO ME GREATLY MULTIPLIED.

—EVERY DAY IN EVERY WAY, MY FINANCIAL WORTH INCREASES.

—I AM INSPIRED TO MAKE MONEY AND TO HAVE MY MONEY MAKE MONEY FOR MYSELF AND EVERYONE ELSE.

—I ENJOY MONEY AND MONEY ENJOYS ME.

—I CREATE MONEY HEALTH WHEN I USE MY MONEY TO ENHANCE MY HEALTH AND

THE HEALTH OF OTHERS, MY COUNTRY
AND MY WORLD.
—I HAVE A POSITIVE CASH FLOW RIGHT
HERE AND RIGHT NOW.
—I AM A CREATIVE MONEY GENERATOR.
—IT IS FUN TO MAKE LOTS OF MONEY.
—I AM A MONEY-MAKING MACHINE.
—ALL OF MY INVESTMENTS ARE PROFI-
TABLE AND BECOMING MORE SO.
—I'LL MAKE IT NO MATTER WHAT!
—I FEEL GOOD ABOUT MONEY (PROSPERITY
AND ABUNDANCE).
—I LIKE MONEY AND I AM NOT ASHAMED TO
ADMIT IT.
—MY MIND IS PROGRAMMED EXCLUSIVELY
TO PROSPERITY.
—I THINK, ACT, WALK, TALK, SMELL AND
LOOK PROSPEROUS.

The basic principle of true prosperity that so
many people need to brand into their brains and
etch into the fabric of their beings is: LIFE IS FOR
US UNCONDITIONALLY. As Dr. Albert Einstein
said: "The basic question is 'Is Universe friendly or
not?'" He decided and said, "Universe is 'friendly.'"
Life is for you and me. It is ready to give us
whatever we claim; whatever we aim for we will
obtain. Most people either aim wrong or not at all
because of ignorance. You will obtain whatever you
aim for, high or low, so aim high now! The fact that
replete abundance is available to everyone equally
then needs only true desire, recognition,
acceptance and use of the same.

Take a personal prosperity self-inventory:

(1) Where you have been with prosperity.

As a child: what did your parents say about
money? What were the attitudes about money that

you had? Your parents had? Your neighborhood had (experienced)? Your teachers had? What was the atmosphere of the nation (depression to boom times on a scale of 1, poor, to 10, rich)?

(2) Where you are now.
Where are you now? Do you really want to be prosperous? You are where you are because that's where you want to be. Ask yourself: "How much can I give away now and still have enough to attend to my wants, needs and desires?" and "How much time, money and effort will I sacrifice to become rich?"

Are you part of the active flow of life? Many people have money but are constipating its flow and theirs. To be truly prosperous, you must know, believe, feel and see that the prosperity experience is at its best as the law of circulation — where you either use it or lose it.

(3) Where you want to be.
Where you want to be is most important. What you have not been, have not done and have not thought is irrelevant. Now is the only time there is, and now is the time to choose future prosperity. Think big, act big and get big results. N-O-W!

The so-called Great Depression of the 1930's was evidence of massive faith in fear. Money is at some levels a myth, and the Depression monitored a collapse of that myth. Individuals lost faith in themselves and the economy. Money continued to exist, it merely changed hands rapidly. Those who thought right about money achieved vast fortunes almost overnight, like Joe Kennedy did because they were mentally ready. The truth is that your state of mind and not the general state of the economy affects your personal financial situation.

Different states of prosperity and poverty exist

always, as do states within the United States. And like driving your car from one state to another, you can leave the state of mind called poverty and drive into prosperity. The choice is yours and yours alone.

Fortunes have been, are, and will continue to be made during recessions and depressions. Don't let the mass-psychosis and media propaganda hypnotize you into believing otherwise. The *Biblical* phrase is " ... he who hath, gets." Hathness, or haveness, is your state of mind. Choose to positively control your state of mind to riches.

The crime in this world is that so many less-developed countries pass on poverty from generation to generation, as America does a welfare system that cripples and demoralizes people. Peter Drucker says there are no under-developed countries or people, only under-managed countries and people. Be a great self-manager. What each of us can do is to make sure these vital principles of prosperity get exposed to the largest possible audiences. Please share this with everyone you know. Write us for quantity discounts.

Prosperity is an inside job, a mental decision. You do not need to depend on another person, place, thing, circumstance or condition. You stimulate or retard the flow of good to you based on your own thinking.

It is helpful to seek counsel, advice and wisdom from someone who is doing what you want to do, who is encouraging and helpful, who decided to do what you can decide to do, i.e., "find a need and fill it," as Bernard Baruch said.

Andrew Carnegie decided, "I'll manufacture and market steel." Inadvertently, he discovered he had to "build people" in the process.

Kemmons Wilson said, "I'll be the world's innkeeper." Today we get a new Holiday Inn room every 14 minutes.

Thomas Alva Edison said, "I'll be the world's greatest inventor." He created 1,097 inventions, only four of which aren't actively used daily. The world needs you to find your need—your talent and ability—and fill it — now!

Prosperity is love, love is prosperity. Prosperity is a positive extension of your personality. You can magnetize yourself to attract more money by loving and enjoying it more. Business people who love the service or product they render are always prosperous to the maximum because to them that service or product is *effortless effort*. It is not a job, it is a creative outlet for their vast and expanding ideas, time, talent and money-making ability.

Positive self-esteem attracts prosperity, while negative self-esteem repels it. Believing you can be prosperous, believing you deserve it, has your mind making prosperous thoughts into things. Thoughts always become things. The objective of Art Bartlett, co-founder of Century 21, was to build the world's biggest real estate franchise. Today, Century 21 does business worth 1% of America's GNP (gross national product), $20-plus billion per year, because of a big dream.

To make the world better, start by making yourself better. Individuals learn by identification, imitation, instruction and example. Choose consciously to start now by identifying with, imitating, being instructed by, reading about and watching examples of prosperous people. Someone earning $10,000 anually cannot teach you how to earn $100,000 yearly or $1,000,000 yearly. Study the rich to get rich. Read books by and about Andrew Carnegie, Thomas Edison, J. Paul Getty,

Aristotle Onassis, John D. Rockefeller, et al.
—I AM THINKING WHAT I WANT TO THINK.
—I AM MENTALLY INDEPENDENT, PHYSI-
   CALLY, EMOTIONALLY AND FAMILIALLY.
—I AM RICH IN EVERY GOOD WAY.
—I AM LOVED AND LOVING.
—I AM QUIETLY EFFECTIVE.
—I AM ALWAYS OPERATING FROM
   STRENGTH.
—I AM A STRONG, SELF-CONFIDENT
   PERSON.
—I SURROUND MYSELF WITH EXCITING,
   ENTHUSIASTIC PEOPLE WHO ARE
   EXPERIENCING THE JOY OF LIFE.

Affirmations

Affirmations are the words you say to yourself
or others say to you that you believe, think about,
act upon and then, that act upon you.

You talk to yourself all the time. Everyone does.
You are either talking yourself up or talking
yourself down. You possess the most incredible
power of all — the power to *choose* what you think.

You may say something as simple as: "I *feel* good
or I *feel* bad." The *choice* is yours. Thoughts are
things. What you think about, you become and
manifest in your experience. It's little *feelings* like the
ones listed above that are the steering wheel of our
future experience. Your present verbal attitude
about yourself is your future in the process of
becoming reality. What words are you constantly
saying about yourself? Are you *choosing* to be a
happy, loving, self-fulfilling, successful,
prosperous person with peace of mind? You can if
your words to yourself and about yourself *say* you
can. Because what you affirm about yourself is
what you get.

Affirmations are mentally ingested in the first person — *I am;* in the second person — *you are;* in the third person — *You, Mark Victor Hansen, are;* in what I call the fourth person — *We (this group) are* . . . These verbal statements voiced in your head mold your potentially creative thinking into limiting or expanding patterns of thought. You have the power of *choice* once you are aware of it. As you read the following, seriously re-think what words you attract to your "I AM."

I AM . . .

"I AM" is the commander of all your thoughts. Whatever words you attach to "I AM" eventually, with verbal repetition, become your experience.

If the little boy who is constantly asked, "What are you going to be when you grow up?" repeatedly says, " I am going to be a doctor," his thought-creating parents positively, reinforcingly say, "You are going to be a doctor." His relatives lovingly approve, saying, "You, Johnny, are going to be a doctor and we need a doctor in our family." With mountains of mental encouragement like this, Johnny becomes a doctor. A minor question is, did Johnny really want to be a doctor?

"I AM"s only work in the eternal *now.* While they cannot currently affect yesterday, they are creators of your Now and all the tomorrows of your life. "I AM"s are too often casual thoughts that become *casual* thoughts.

The words you add to "I AM" are your self-definition in process. "I AM"s are your self-affirming brainwashing. The words following "I AM" define you. Pick yourself up mentally with positive "I AM"s.

Your thoughts proceed you. Positive-growth "I AM"s inspire you, but negative "I AM"s expire you. Are you green and growing or ripe and rotting?

The learning process proceeds by identification, imitation, example and instruction. The words in this book are teaching you by instruction. Additionally, you choose either to instruct yourself in the self-actualizing "I AM"s of life or to find outstanding individuals, alive or transitioned, with whom you can identify and imitate.

I AM...
Choose the I AM you *want*, not necessarily the one you are using.

> *POSITIVE*
> Lean, slim, trim,
> physically fit
> Intelligent
> Just right
> Happy
> Healthy
> Successful
> Prosperous
> Loving
> Rich and elegant
>
>
> *NEGATIVE*
> too fat
> stupid
> too tall or too short
> unhappy, sad, miserable
> sick, diseased
> failure
> poor, broke,
> suffering,
> deprived
> unloved
> a fat cat

WHO/WHAT IS TO BLAME
Mom, Dad, heredity,
fast foods, bakeries
neighbors, friends,
parents, teacher said so
God, genetics, parents,
milk, cigarettes
the economy, parents,
lover, friends, job,
children
environment, heredity,
diet, weather, etc.
teachers, relatives,
money, contacts
neighborhood, job,
no opportunity
appearance, mouthwash,
luck, parents
taxes, crooks, cheats,
liars, government

Try to choose a life-fulfilling set of I AM words that best describe the strengths, talents, skills and abilities that affirm the person you are and *want to become*. Here are more than 50 starter words. Develop your own list. Add at least a word a day. Glance at it daily, pondering a select word throughout an entire day. Notice grouping of adjectives even promotes a healthier self-image.

I AM...

These are my strengths, assets, skills and abilities:

Healthy	Wealthy
Happy	Assertive
Successful	Sincere
Prosperous	Helpful
Calm	Strong
Intelligent	Alive

Turned on	A millionaire
Loved & Loving	A billionaire
Generous	Exciting
Useful	Excited
Purposeful	Enthusiastic
Decisive	Self-reliant
Beautiful	Self-created
Special	Self-image builder
Unique	A people builder
God's greatest miracle	Thoughtful
A writer	Thought-filled
A reader	A goal setter
A great speaker	A goal getter
A positive person	Joy-filled
A possibility thinker	Joyous
A confident person	A giver & receiver
A competent person	A good person
A thinker	Wise
A saver	Earning lots of money
Physically fit	A bill payer
Rich & elegant	Wonderful
Persistent	

One success-philosopher became a millionaire by saying, "I AM a millionaire already, I just have to go out and collect it."

Chapter Four
The Extra I AM

The Extra I AM

Chip Collins once told me that continuous reading of a selected book is an affirmation. He and I, and many others, have been inspired and re-inspired by Napoleon Hill's *Think & Grow Rich*. We've addressed this text until it affirmatively permeates our consciousness. It is branded into our brains and etched into the fabric of our beings.

Scientists do this with science books. Artists do this with art books, politicians with political manifestos, Christian devotees with the *Bible*. With what "extra I AM" book(s) are you sculpting your mind?

Positive "I AM"s

Positive "I AM"s are constantly and continuously repeated by individuals who are being something, doing something and having something. Artists, inventors, scientists, mothers, fathers, sons and daughters use affirmations. You are I AMing yourself instantly and constantly.

Let's learn from success in different endeavors:

Athletics: Mohammad Ali—Ten years ago he seemed like a loudmouth screaming, "I am the greatest." Now we know that he was disciplining his mind wisely and well, and he harvested the world's heavyweight boxing title along with respect, admiration and world renown.

Business: J. Paul Getty, multi-billionaire and the world's richest man, wrote in his autobiography *As I See It*: "I am rich and I have always felt that I had a reserved seat in life.... I take pride in the creation of wealth, in its existence and in the uses to which it has been and is being put ... it is invested and at work ... it makes possible the production of goods and services for millions of consumers and provides well-paid employment for some 12,000 people in the United States, Great Britain, Europe, The Middle East, Japan and other parts of the world..."

Writing: Dr. Wayne W. Dyer, author of *Your Erroneous Zones*, expected and visualized himself as author of America's number-one, record-breaking best-seller. Then he went out and achieved his ambition in a remarkably short time. After reading that mind-expanding book, attend one of Dyer's live talks if you can—you'll be glad you did. He speaks on how to live an effective, self-actualizing life, and his own life admirable provides an example of his points. He *wanted* a best-selling book, then convinced an editor on a "cold call" to buy the concept. He wrote *Your Erroneous Zones* in 17 days, spent four months promoting it, wanted to be on Johnny Carson's T.V. show and appeared there a number of times. His life is the success he chooses it to be now. Is yours?

Money Choices

You can fear or love money. Experience teaches that it's better to correctly and positively love money and welcome it into your experience.

Rich people are often more loving and productive for society than poor people, so why not choose riches?

Gaining prosperity requires no hard work or extraordinary sacrifices, only a properly conditioned mind. Why not condition yours?

Enjoyment of your prosperity increases your prosperity. Emotional health facilitates healthy, prosperous attitudes. Most of us began our lives imbibing our parents' money scripts and have never thoughtfully examined them in light of the insights shared herein.

Financial satisfaction is a desirable, believable and attainable goal for everyone and may be better than financial independence. If our regular desires are totally taken care of with $25,000, $50,000, $100,000 or $250,000 annually, who needs $5,000,000 annually? Think through your financial satisfaction and financial independence needs, wants and desires. If you had twice as much money coming in weekly as you could spend, what would you do with it?

Giving

You can't receive unless you give and you can't give unless you have received. The truth of giving is that you have something to give.

To really experience prosperity, you have got to rid yourself of guilt—guilt about having money and guilt about wanting money. Money is good, it is not bad. It is especially good when it is a servant of right thinking, right stewardship, right action and right results. Your mind has the ability to direct money use positively and correctly. Do it.

Guilt comes from a low self-image, the belief that you are undeserving of wealth, the belief that you are unworthy of abundance. It comes out of misunderstanding and misinformation. You must consciously choose to create and maintain a money consciousness. Affirm to yourself, silently, "I like money and I am not ashamed to admit it."

Inferiority also stifles and stops the money flow to you. Overcome inferiority with right desire and right action. Dale Carnegie overcame his feelings of shyness and inferiority by forcing himself to speak in public. Once he learned the art of oral communication he taught it. The Dale Carnegie Institute, his namesake, continues to teach what he learned and taught, and it takes in millions yearly. If you have inferiority or shyness problems about your self-image, I totally recommend you enroll in Carnegie classes.

Unconscious fears about money scare money away. A consciouness that is not conditioned repetitively and positively to welcome prosperity and abundance automatically repels them. Are you attracting or repelling your own prosperity?

Life's Security

Life has no favorites. Rather, conscious people are people who choose to be self-determining. They are street-smart, have common sense, and do not believe in lack during good times or bad times. They know that the flow of good is as available to them as to anyone, all the time, because the universe exists and everything in it regenerates—always.

Most individuals have grown up seeing, feeling and believing in limitation and have subconsciously assumed that that's the way it is and that they'll have to live with it. The truth is that you obtain in the outer world whatever you consistently picture inside your mind.

Individuals are so negative that they don't even know they are negative when they say, "I'll never have enough money, my job is my security, I'm just a poor person, I can't afford it, I'm too young or old, I'm stifled by my spouse. And if only I had this or that, I could earn more, be more, do more and have more."

Security exists only in your mind. Security is not the dollars you have in the bank or invest in business or rental properties. *Security is the thoughts you have in your mind.* Security is a self-generated inside job, created inside your mind. In this incarnation, you exist behind the only eye-balls you will be behind and in the only bag of skin you will have. Choose to be secure. As you increase your security of mind, you will choose work you love rather than work you do only for money. And the truth is that doing work you love will facilitate rapid self-advancement and probably higher earnings, too.

All the wealth in the world will not buy, nor be a sufficient substitute for love, family, spiritual fulfillment and the real satisfaction of having a meaningful purpose in life.

Prosperity is! If it's not for you, who is it for? Your participation in prosperity makes available more prosperity, not less. As an example, it's been figured by insurance company actuarials that a salesperson earning $20,000-plus annually employs 14 other people directly or indirectly. You owe it to yourself and others to earn, circulate, save, invest, and tithe high quantities of money. The law of circulation states that money carries the highest moral good when its flow generates more money for everyone because it's an energy that, when stifled and made to stagnate, withers and dies from lack of use. Whenever you circulate a dollar, visualize it going out in multiple service doing its necessary good and returning itself to you in various ways from time to time, multiplied and increased in every good way. This will eradicate any hoarding tendencies you may have and open your heart to generosity and the understanding of good money-movement. Many people have lots of money and ignorantly hoard it. I read about a postal employee in Durango, Colorado, who looked and acted like a beggar. People forever were giving this man handouts because he paid for everything with quarters. After his death, $88,000 cash was found in his apartment, hidden under the carpet and in the bed. I daresay he never enjoyed money.

One success-philosopher encourages us to write "E.R."= 10 times on every check we write. "E.R." means equal return. What he means is that every time you pay a bill, be thankful for your ability to pay the bill. In your mind, you'll positively want to pay for services previously rendered (i.e., telephone service, rent, credit cards, et al). You'll feel good rather than bad about paying your bills off and up, because more good will circulate to you. You'll feel good and go out and declare new things and create them in your experience. It will be wonderful and you will be mentally secure. That's what prosperity thinking is all about.

Total Prosperity Ideas

You have the unlimited ability to choose. You have the under-used capacity to choose every second in favor of what you want or don't want, what you'll be or won't be, what you'll have or won't have, and, most importantly, what you'll think or won't think.

Life is most pleasant when you choose from the vast and ever-increasing array of omnipresent opportunities. These opportunities expand fastest when you are mentally positive, open, actively thinking, doing, being and having the good you desire.

Your Occupation

You can have an exciting, interesting occupation. When I realized the truth of this idea, I started my own speaking business. I knew who the best speakers in the world were and I *decided* to become one of them. I decided to *enjoy the price of becoming.* I looked at all the opportunities each individual had looked at and *decided* to *create* my own space. I started booking myself at an insurance-agency level, where no one had ever tried to sell seminars before. I started at below market price, charging only $25 per hour to talk. Since then, as my knowledge, experience, expertise, reputation and self-image have grown, so have my fees. And there is no end in sight. (Note: Your every desire contains intrinsic to it, the mechanics that will show you how to enter into whatever occupation or business you want in an affordable way—starting where you are and moving onward, upward and Godward.) You, too, can *choose* an occupation and get turned on to "how-to's" by your predecessors or develop your own new, unique and different niche, as I did. I created what I *wanted.*

The only individual who can change my occupation is me. If I want something more, better, greater and different, I choose it in my mind. You, too, have the greatest power of all—the power to *choose in your mind,* right here and now, what you want. Write down what you want—*with all your heart*—on a piece of paper, then implant those desires in your mind. As you grow and develop, keep writing down more. I AM and it's working. I feel, as I hope you do, that my life is great now and is going to be getting better and better. As the saying goes, "You ain't seen nothing yet." That's true—if you see your future big, beautiful and bountiful in your *mind* now. I do. Do you? Ben Feldman, one of the world's best salesmen, once was asked, "What's your best sale?" He answered, "I haven't made it yet." Likewise, Woody Allen says he has not made his best film yet. Realize your best and noblest endeavor is before you.

Your Marriage

You can choose to have a good marriage. Choose an idealistic, romantic, life-filling marriage and mate. Write down what would make your marriage perfect. Read good love-marriage books and sex manuals. Expand your human-relations awareness, marital creativity and choose in favor of the joy of loving. The more thriving (prosperous) your love considerations and thoughts are, the more love you will attract into your experience.

Your Friends

In your dream-like meditative state, choose the exciting, interesting, influential, powerful, productive, high-consciousness friends you would like to have. Write down the names of 50 people whom you want to become your friends. I wrote down a list of 200 names of individuals world-around that I wanted to meet and progressively I have met them. I am forever adding more names to my list and writing "victory" behind the names of those I've met. This principle is magic. Do it now!

Many I thought would be difficult to meet have been easy, friendly and oftentimes even extraordinarily hospitable, offering me weekend lodging at their great estates. It's amazing how easy this has been. It's true: good human relations start with you. Take an interest in someone special—study them, read about them, listen to their tapes, watch their films and, if possible, write them or ask your friends or their friends to introduce you. I state in my Sunshine Seminars that you're never more than three people away from anyone who's living whom you know you want to meet. The first question is: "Who do you want to meet?" The second question, which has part of its answer in the first, is: "What are three ways I could meet him or her?" Then: "Which is the best way?" Then: "Do it—now!"

Using this technique, I have met great actors, speakers, artists, inventors, scientists, gurus, spiritual leaders and a never-ending chain of individuals who excite me and whom I excite to a more inspired, rich, self-filling life.

Your Home or Estate

The choice of where you live is yours. It's important to know that your environment can uplift you if it's good, energizing and beautiful. It is my belief that everyone desires an enjoyable environment that facilitates a complete lifestyle. That desire made conscious, backed by a committed decision and a positive self-demand, could give everyone continually better external spaces to live in and be enlivened by.

Having a home or homes, an estate or estates, an apartment or apartments, starts as everything does, in your mind. As you think about it you'll see that what others have done you can do too. Visit the great ones. Visit Frank Lloyd Wright's two estates, Taliesin West in Phoenix, Arizona, and Taliesin East in Wisconsin. Visit many great estates and read the stories about how they were started. Wright started with an inspired idea and no money. He started as an inspired architect who attracted interest and discovered his own great abilities in architectural artistry. Others who could see his vision funded him. Dr. Robert Schuller says of this principle: "Make a positive decision first, then solve the problem."

Where do you want to reside? You can choose the location you want, the type of residence, who you want to build it, and with whom you want to live. This may fit under long-range goals which are spoken of in another chapter. Only one thing is for sure: if you decide now to write nothing, plan for nothing—you'll get nothing. But if you have the courage to choose the future apartment(s), home(s), estate(s) or mansion(s) of your choice— YOU CAN HAVE THEM. Happy dwelling.

Your Free Time

You choose to invest or squander your time today so you can experience more or less of it in the tomorrows of your life.

Countless students of mine have written down that they wanted, within three years, to work in their jobs only nine months per year and work on themselves three months per year. One couple I know works nine months and lives in Mexico the other three months of the year. They were kind enough to entreat me to spend two weeks with them in the winter of 1977. I thoroughly enjoyed it. I discovered that by no choice you'll get to work fifty-plus weeks per year like everyone else. The unchoosing majority, however, by abstractly choosing more free time, your mind will discover ways and means to be more productive in less time, so you can "work on yourself—which is the only work there is," in your reinvestible free time.

Another friend decided to work nine months per year and vacation three months per year in a mobile home with his family. This goal inspired him to become one of the world's best insurance salespeople and a much better father and family man.

Choosing the amount of free time you want inspires you to coordinate your other objectives so that everything is accomplished on time.

Your Travel

Doing what you want to do, when you want to do it, is a good operational definition of prosperity.

Most amateur demonstrators would venture to say prosperity for them means fine automobiles, fine homes, luxuries and travel. I love to travel. I have been around the world four times and expect to go 400-plus times more. I fly more than 250,000 miles annually, the equivalent of 10 annual around-the-world trips. I intimately know my way around most of America's key cities and many internationally important cities like Montreal, London, Bombay, Guadalajara and Ocho Ricos.

What I've discovered is that travel is fun, thrilling and edifying. Everyone has a birthright to partake extensively of our Garden of Eden called Earth. Consciousness makes it so, when the heart is willing and wanting. "So be it done unto you!" Obviously, the places, transportation, people and so on are, as Delta Airline advertises, "ready when you are." So instantly write out a list of all the fine places you want to take yourself, your family and others—life treats you like you treat yourself.

Travel ideas and choices will get you traveling. Traveling is available to everyone, always. Most people, however, remain standing at the counter of life, saying "take me." The question is: Where do you want to go? When? By what means? With whom? At what cost? I choose to go places and then my clients underwrite the expense. You have the same power to choose a place. Keep dreaming positively about it and creating the reason why someone else should invest in your experience. Write down 10 places you want to go. Visit the library and study them. Check with your travel agent for brochures. Hang travel posters on your walls. Ponder them and believe you will go, and soon, almost as if by magic, you'll be there.

As some of you are reading this treatise on prosperity, you're saying: "This is too good to be true. It can't be this simple. I just can't believe it." Well, all of those statements are negative and work to deny your own prosperity. You can't deny subconsciously what you affirm in consciousness and get the appropriate results. If your feeling nature and sense of self-worth believe wrongly, then prosperity cannot join itself to your experience. Often being open and receptive to travel will result in your winning unexpected bonus trips—ask around and you will be amazed how one in 10 Americans has won one or more free trips. Imagine yourself in that reality.

Joe Gandolfo, the world's best salesman, chooses to work hard four days per week, 10-plus hours per day and spend three full days per week with his family in Lakeland, Florida.

The choice of how much free time you want, and when, is yours. Believe it, choose it, and you'll have it.

Thoughtsmanship

You are here to celebrate. You are here to experience abundance and joy in your individuality. Freedom of mind is your birthright.

Average individuals have 1,000 thoughts each day and live 72-plus years. Thus, each one has 1,000 thoughts $\times$ 365 days $\times$ 72 years, equaling 26,280,000 thoughts in his or her lifetime. What do you want from your 26 million thoughts? You have the ability to cultivate and harvest as many or as few of your thoughts as you like. You determine the quality and quantity of your thinking by your choices. You can choose. Choose to have a PMA (Positive Mental Attitude which Pays More

*A*lways), choose to be a goal setter and goal getter, choose to organize your thoughts, choose to contribute something great to humanity.

Most individuals, unaware of the unlimited power of choice and their own unending flow of ideas, give too much life for too little good. Everything you want wants you, if you'll get those thoughts in your mind and actualize them.

Education

Education is self-acquired. It comes through the development and use of the mind. Mind power is the only power. It comes before all other power. Without mind power, there is no power. Mind alone can harness great lakes, rivers and falls like Niagara Falls and shunt their vast energy into life-benefitting channels. Education is chosen by your *wants*. If you want it, you can have it. Great teachers, libraries, classes and minds exist, waiting and wanting you to enduce them, which literally means to draw them out. What education are you choosing now?

You create opportunities for yourself. The greatest tragedy in your life is to think you have no choices, no options. You always have choices. Your future choices expand as you choose to be more, do more and live more. There is a use and disuse principle: if you don't use your lifetime of choices *when they come up*, you lose them. Use 'em or lose 'em.

The mother of Ray Charles, the black musician, taught him he always had three choice ways to solve every problem. Once he stated the three choices, she'd ask: "Which one's best? ... Let's do that now." What are your three choices to every problem?

When you believe as Mrs. Charles did that you always have three choices, you make a priority decision that *creates* psychic space for three choices.

It expands the visibility of choices and options by belief.

The mind-blowing truth about choice is that *there is only supply.* Nature's table is ever filled and totally abundant. There is exactly as much in your experience as you choose there to be. If you choose rich ideas, you'll manifest riches. Choose healthy ideas and you manifest health.

Dr. Fuller chose to think as a world-citizen and envisioned a 100% successful humanity. His provocative ideas are now being adopted, exercised and actualized by others. For instance, slightly less than half of humanity is now starving because we have not humanely chosen a big enough idea to feed everyone. The gross amount of edible food in the equatorial belt around the earth is more than sufficient to nourish every human alive comprehensively, as well as those to be born between now and the year 2000. The fact is that a problem can't get solved until *someone* or some group(s) are concentrating on it. That *someone* could be you—if you choose to *think* about the matter positively. Ideas are the unlimited real-capital asset of everyone. You get them, harvest them, write them down and *actualize* them to the betterment of yourself and everyone else. As you *choose* big ideas, your real mind starts to think/work, and it will connect you with infinite intelligence (God) which will be forever whispering more ideas into your growingly capable mind.

Money

Money goes to ideas and ideas always and always create money. How much money do you *want* to make or spend in the following areas?

(Write the amounts in NOW. This is your book.)

I. Income:

A. Earning-power income:

(Special note: If you earned $100,000 in the past year, given 20% inflation, you need to earn $140,000 to stay even in the next year in a 50% tax bracket. That's a *40% increase*, so be generous in your growth expectations. Don't be limited by past or present circumstances. If you earn over $31,000 per year after deductions, you're in a 50% tax bracket and will work for Uncle Sam until mid-June.)

B. Net-worth income (investments):

(Special note: 1) Read: *Wall Street Journal* on Wednesdays; "Tax-Tips" 2) Read: *Master Tax Guide* available for $2.50 from Commerce Clearing House, Inc., Chicago, Illinois.

1. Now: _____

2. In 5 years: _____

3. In 10 years: _____

4. In 25 years: _____

II. Retirement: _____

III. Car(s): _____

Kind(s): _____

Price(s): _____

IV. Homes plus investments in real property:

V. Children's Education:

VI. Life Insurance (including Keogh, IRA, health, disability, et al): _____

VII. Banks (deposits and kinds of financial instruments): (Interview a savings and loan banker, a commercial banker and a credit union director for insights into what is available.)

VIII. Art, antiques and other collectibles: (Write out a list of the artists whose works you want to own, i.e., Dali, Rockwell, Austin, et al)

IX. Gold, Silver, Diamonds:

(Start with personal accessories, i.e., gold rings and diamond-studded watches, et al)

X. Your own business:

XI. Stocks, bonds and mutual funds:

XII. Other:

Where Choice Starts

Choice starts in your mind. You choose mentally what you want to manifest materially. The ABC of success, written in the first person, is: I'll *Always Be Choosing*. There is no great and no small—you have the choice to choose all!

Your consciousness cannot execute thought until you choose something. You can experience greater good because you can conceive it. Mind chooses and thereby governs experience. Self-choice and self-belief in that choice determine the expansiveness or limitation of demonstration of our choices. The invisible *cause* of all is choice. When you *recognize the power of choice*, you choose more, conceive more, believe more and achieve more. Accept more in conscious choice and you'll experience more. Congratulations, chooser!

You Are Always on the Way

Goals, once attained, are no longer so important. Therefore, you must constantly set and re-set goals that turn you on.

Getting promoted, winning a gold metal, going on a trip, meeting someone important—all these are fantastic. Achievement of a goal necessitates a new goal, because satisfaction is short-lived. Remember to savor and relish each memorable experience as you live it. As the cliche goes, "Smell the flowers along the way."

If you are not going somewhere specific, you are not going at all. Vague and wandering goals get vague and wandering results.

There are no endings.
Everything is a process:
Ideas processing into ideas,
Actions processing into other actions,
Love processing into love.
Are you part of the active flow of life? Many
people have money, but they constipate its flow and
theirs. To be truly prosperous, you must know,
believe, feel and see that the prosperity experience
is at its best as the law of circulation, where you
either use it or lose it.

Affirmations

Affirmations are the words you say to yourself
or others say to you that you believe, think about,
act upon and then, that act upon you. Whatever
your dominating inner-dialog of affirmations is,
you are becoming. Listen to yourself analytically
but not condemningly or judgmentally. If your
money thoughts are negative in orientation,
reverse them. If you have been thinking negatively
for 31 years, it will take time to change. It takes time
to change your thinking, but the rewards are
enormous and the pay-off is millions of dollars. You
have the greatest money-making machine ever
devised in the universe: your brain and mind,
waiting for you to discover and use them. Your
brain is computer-like in its ability to hold, store
and retrieve information. Your mind is magnificent
in its ability to think and consciously direct itself,
you, your actions, and others too. Your mind is only
slightly less able than God's.

The Prosperity Proclamations to actuate your
subconscious are:
—"I am rich!"
—"I desire and deserve large quantities of money."
—"I am a money magnet."
—"More and more money is coming to me easily

and effortlessly."

—"I think positively and correctly about money. It's rushing to me from expected and unexpected sources."

—"Money loves me and I love money."

—"Money is my servant, I do not serve money."

—"I see all of my bills paid off and up, and still I have all that money."

—"Money is good, especially in its rightful place ... bulging in my pockets, bank accounts and interest-bearing investments."

There is an absolute abundance of prosperity awaiting your recognition and acceptance. To accept that abundance, if you don't have it or haven't ever experienced it, takes reprogramming of your fundamental life-tapes and subconscious imprints and impressions. You must choose consciously to start and constantly continue to "be rich" by thinking, feeling, believing and imaging your growing prosperity. Think of it as fun. Embrace ideas of prosperity with a loving heart and you will attract prosperity with accelerating acceleration. Progressively as your belief system releases you from the bondage of have-not-ness, you achieve more haveness. Haveness is a conditioned reflex of mental acceptance. You are the one who must condition your reflexes. It's your right to be rich. It's a birthright. A rich state of mind is normal and natural and available by right thinking. Your thoughts need only be directed and made to be prosperity-minded.

Unconsciously, many people are afraid of money. They are not sure they could trust themselves if they had too much money. Yet money, at its best, creates jobs and happiness, and it facilitates love, home, hospitals, schools, parks, libraries, etc.

Money-conscious individuals will tell you that they got theirs by thinking in larger terms. When you think big, you get big results. As a child you probably thought $10 was a lot. Add one zero and you have $100, which to a beginning worker may be a lot. As your business prospers and you personally enjoy the laws of growth, you keep adding zeros to grow to $1,000, $10,000, $100,000, $1,000,000, etc. The infinite doesn't care whether you want to be a zip, a millionaire or a billionaire. Universe will not force your good on you—you must choose it. My opinion is, we need more individuals to be truly self-reliant and test how much they can create.

An enlarged idea about your prosperity can only bring enlarged results. However, don't pre-spend it unless you've got great cash-flow, or the net effect is psychological debt, fear, and ultimately the opposite effect from what you are attempting to achieve.

To uplift your prosperity consciousness, teach prosperity to someone else who wants to know the laws of prosperity. Motivating others will encourage and motivate you. Dr. Norman Vincent Peale once asked me: "Do you know who leaves a motivational seminar the most motivated?"

I responded enthusiastically: "Yes, I do." (I am a professional motivational speaker.) Just visualize how wonderfully the world could work if everyone knew and actively used the laws of prosperity. Toward that worthy end, and as a gift to yourself, please share this treatise with 12 of your best friends.

Chapter Five
Tithing Works

Tithing Works

Tithing works. It works when you work it, as any principle or system does. And tithing is a principle that, when systematically used, gives regular, systematic ten- hundred- or thousand-fold returns, dependent upon your belief system.

In Hebrew the word "tithe" means tenth. It means to give one-tenth of *all* your income back to your spiritual source, God. Students of truth know, as Christ said, that, "The Kingdom of Heaven (God and good) is within you." It's true that God is in you. It's further true that most of us come to acknowledge that God-is-in-me through an external source, usually a church, minister, person, book, tape, TV show or radio program. Occasionally someone's mediation facilitates this truth. Because that source facilitated your (growing) awareness of who you are in God and who God is in you, you have a spiritual obligation with your source to finance (tithe) and help perpetuate the spiritual messages that sustained you. Whatever you contribute to, contributes back to you. The return is not onefold, but minimally tenfold (Old Testament, Malachi 3:10), hundred fold (New Testament, Mark 10:29) or thousand-fold as witnessed in the story of the loaves and fishes (New Testament). The Lord (Law of Mind) promises a multiplied return to come "according to your faith."

Consider: "Give, and it shall be given unto you; good measure, pressed down, and shaken together, and running over, shall men give into your bosom. For with the same measure that ye mete withal it shall be measured to you again" (Luke 6:38).

What that scripture means is that God multiplies back to you *all* that you give. He gives you 100% in trust, faith and loving understanding. Recognize and realize the karmic law of tithing: "...as you sow, so shall you reap..." A tithe is an investment, in which one invests 10% to get a 100% return and then some. You cannot over-use this principle. It seems to work best when you are habituated to it.

Throughout the Old Testament we discover that the tithing covenant was obligatory. There was no choice. It was a requirement much like the taxation levied by the U.S. government. When Christ stimulated the New Testament and a new tithing covenant, however, he said tithing should be done in the spirit of love. The Lord loveth a cheerful giver. Christ intimated that individuals who love will love to give their tithings and offerings and will do so knowing their return will be multiplied.

Tithing has four main aspects:
1) Consciousness
2) Effort
3) Time
4) Money

Give (tithe) 10% of your *consciousness*. Christ said, "The Father and I are one!" God (consciousness) is your source and supply of all good. Dr. Emmett Fox said, "Consciousness is life." Truth students know that God is consciousness. He is the original intelligence and creator. In the first commandment we discover: "I am the Lord (Law of Mind) thy God, thou shalt have no others before me."

"I AM" is all the consciousness you will ever have in this incarnation. You can do as much or as little with it as you choose, for God can do no more for you than He can do through you. It behooves you to get psychologically centered, to feel your true spiritual nature, beingness and full personhood, and to acknowledge and commune with the God-in-you. Psalm 1:3 says, "...and whatsoever he doeth shall prosper." You will come to know that the resources of the infinite are infinite. Give (tithe) 10% of your daily thinking to God. Think God's good, loving, beautiful, peaceful and harmonious thoughts about yourself, your loved ones, your enemies, others, the world and the universe. It will help you to employ with creativity the amazing tool you possess called "mind," which is what you think with and through. To be fully human, one must be aware of his or her deep and penetrating spiritual nature.

Give (tithe) 10% of your *effort*. When you give some of your effort-energies to God, probably through the vehicle of your church, your life flows. I say "probably" because the great book, *Try Giving Yourself Away*, by David Dunne, will teach you many ways to do it. You will enjoy effortless effort in everything else you do. Christ (consciousness) said, "My yoke is easy, my burden is light," and it is when—not if—you follow simple tithing principles of life. These principles never go on vacation, never go out of season, never become obsolete, never work for one person and not another. They are true, automatic and immutable. They work when you work them. Offer your effort-energy freely and generously to your church and stand back for an extraordinary return. I've witnessed love affairs that manifest themselves as beautiful marriages as just one of many seemingly miraculous results. It works.

Give (tithe) 10% of your *time*. Time is the vital stuff of life. You have all that exists for anyone. Each of us gets 24 non-refundable fragments of eternity magically filling his or her purse every day to use or misuse, as we choose. Most misuse and misappropriate time because they forget or were never told to tithe time. If you want more time, tithe it.

Christ said, "Whom of you by being anxious (about time) can add one cubit to his life?" You can't. You've got all that is, which is the same equal treatment for everyone. However, this gift you were given called time carries on it a tithing-principle price tag that has been inadvertently neglected. You can change that now, and change your life for more abundance totally, by simply tithing time. What this does is to open your consciousness to becoming more creative and effective. Congratulations!

Give (tithe) 10% of your *money*. People who give always have abundance, for the gift of giving is receiving. Giving is, was and always will be a statement of haveness. Christ said, "From him to whom much is given much is required." Everyone has more than they use, because getting disciplined to acknowledge and USE principles makes everything evermore available for you to use. It is normal and natural to be rich. As the 23rd Psalm states: "The Lord (Law of Mind) is my shepherd, *I SHALL NOT WANT*." The Law of Mind is the stuff between idea and manifestation. When you work within the law positively and correctly, it always works with and for you. Ignorance is no excuse. If you have any lack in your life, look again at the law and ask: "Am I tithing?" A scripture in the Book of Genesis says: "As long as the earth remains, there shall be a seed time and a harvest." Whatsoever you sow, you reap. Plant your seeds now to guarantee a harvest. If you are giving right, you will be receiving right. If you are not receiving right, go back to step one—consciousness—and inquire of yourself: "Am I thinking right and giving right?" Christ said, "Your every idle thought . . . shall be judgment day." This means mind is causal. When you give generously, creatively and lovingly your returns are in kind. Never stop giving and you will never stop receiving. Each of us has an intrinsic need, want and desire to give. It is one of the truths of life. When you give your financial support to dissemination of the truth, you are no less than a trustee for humanity's positive growth and development.

Giving is investing—investing in God, who guarantees all returns. As Christ said, when you ". . . give in private, God will reward you openly." Your tithes must be to God's spiritual work. Giving, no matter how nobly, to a cause or philanthropy that is not spiritual is not tithing. Giving is worthy and wonderful. It should be done, and to comply correctly with the law, your giving must be beyond the 10% or more that you have already contributed to your source of spiritual enlightenment and growth.

What most individuals misunderstand about tithing is that *they give either by giving or not giving.* As you give, you will receive abundantly. However, if you do not give, it will be taken back from you in terms of lost opportunities, promotions, increases and blessings, and you will lose some of what you have. Malachi 3:11 says, "And I will rebuke the devourer for your sakes, and he shall not destroy the fruits of your ground; neither shall your vine cast her fruit before the time in the field, saith the Lord of hosts." That's a guarantee of spiritual protection—call it insurance. Curiously enough, every culture throughout all of history has practiced spiritual tithing because it is a universal principle.

Tithing, the giving of 10%, should be done individually and collectively: as a person and as a family, or as an individual and as a company or organization. This simply means that children can and should be encouraged to tithe from their personal allowance and/or earnings beyond what the parental-family unit contributes.

Malachi 3:8 in the Bible says, "If you are not tithing you are robbing God." The only person you can ever steal from is yourself. By not tithing you are robbing yourself of life's abundance and blessings "... in ways you know not of."

Malachi 3:10 says, "Bring all your tithes into the storehouse, that there may be meat (substance) in mine, and prove me now herein, saith the Lord of hosts, if I will not open you the windows of Heaven and pour you out a blessing that *there shall not be room enough to receive it.*"

Wow! That's a powerful promise. It says, "Bring all your tithes!" Not some, not what's left over after you pay bills and taxes, not what's figured from your net income but from your gross income. The law requests and you must self-require and self-discipline yourself to give 10% of *ALL* your income. Often we have subtle income like gifts, bonuses, home appreciation or refinancing, etc., that we forget to tithe. Then, whammo—the law is always working and the excess turns into lack. What was loads and lots becomes lack and overspending simply because we inadvertently forgot to abide in consciousness (1) to remember to give money (4).

The word "storehouse" in Malachi refers to the fact that 2,000-plus years ago when that prophetic message was recorded, the Hebrew nation lived an agricultural existence. The people then brought meat, crops and seeds back into the storehouse. Today, those foodstuffs would translate for most of us into financial tithes from all our earning sources given to the church.

For doing the above, God says, "Prove me!" This means prove to yourself that God multiplies whatever you give. Try it for three months and you will do it forever. He tests you by saying, "Try me, tithe 10%," and He will "open to you the windows of Heaven and pour (that inexhaustible, limitless flow) you out a blessing (higher spiritual states of mind and beingness, happiness, love, joy, success and more money) that there shall not be room enough to receive it." Your cup "RUNNETH over." You will have surpluses, abundance and plenty — and that's the way it should be. Christ took a few fish and created many, and then said, " ... go thou and do likewise!"and, "I have overcome the world." He overcame lack, limitation, shortage, fears, doubts and insecurity of every kind. You can too, but no one can do your doing for you. You must give.

It's obvious that if you are not receiving what you really want out of life then you are holding back what belongs to the universe. Life's only value is in its use. Use it or lose it. Right now, tithe 10% of whatever your most recent income was. Stretch out on God's ability to give through you. Pledge

10% of whatever you would like and love to earn this year and see if, as you work with tithing, tithing doesn't work with you to give you your true place where everything flows to you. You will live, love, laugh and enjoy God's light within showing radiantly without. You will literally feel, believe, and see yourself moving effortlessly from success to success. As Paul said in his letter to the Philippians 4:19: "My God shall supply all your needs according to his abundant riches."

Your gift of giving is receiving. God is looking forward to you receiving more than you ever did before. Congratulations!

Joshua 1:8 says: "Thou shalt make thy way prosperous and then thou shalt have good success."

Chapter Six
Money Beliefs

Money Beliefs

Each individual has over one-hundred money beliefs resident in his or her consciousness. Those beliefs are implanted and impregnated our minds, very subtly, by our parents, relatives, teachers and peers. Beliefs become things and take form in our lives. Therefore, it is necessary and proper to explore what, consciously and unconsciously, we believe. Each of us must edit and erase from our thinking and feelings nature, those beliefs which are clearly not benefiting us. We transplant old beliefs with new ones by thoughtful visualization, verbalization, imagination and actions that give us results.

We discover what we really believe by looking at our actions. Its our beliefs that stimulate our actions, so when you change your belief, you change your actions. Let's explore a few of our most prevelant beliefs.

1. "Money is dirty."

Money is dirty only to a mind that has been polluted to believe that it's dirty. Paper money is re-issued brand new in the U.S.A. every 18 months.

Obviously, money enjoys rapid and frequent circulation from hand to hand, cash register to cash register, pocket to purse to bank. It flows regularly, often changing places as much as 50 times in a single day. That's the tangible, feel-able money of which we are speaking.

Your intangible concept — or idea — about money either facilitates your having more of it or less of it. Most of us are mentally and psychically conditioned not to want that which is not clean. Therefore, in the evolution of commercing with money, some applied-psychologist businessman probably said, "Money's dirty . . . spend it with me now and get a product that's clean." The individual espousing this seemingly harmless little strategy had no idea that his concept would spread like a prairie fire on a windy day and create confusion in other individuals' subconsious as to whether they wanted to possess something dirty, especially large quantities of dirty stuff. The psychological overtones make some folks *feel* bad towards money.

Rather, remember that paper money is a means of exchange and it works to facilitate your most expedient commercing activities. If your hands get dirty, wash them. If your concept of money it dirty — if you possess the "ol' filthy lucre" consciousness — wash and purify that, too. Transform and renew your thinking about money so that you can easily and effortlessly welcome money into your experience. Welcome an abundance of M-O-N-E-Y.

The wrong mental attitude about money, namely, that "it's dirty," will give you the wrong result — less than enough money. You desire to have it overflowing in your experience, or you wouldn't be reading this book. As you amass enough of it, you can be like the late Nelson Rockefeller, the late President John F. Kennedy or

Mrs. Jackie Onassis: you will merely choose whatever it is you would like to acquire and have one of your aides pay for it. Your personal aides will work out the details of transportation, delivery and payment. It's said that Nelson Rockefeller never carried any cash on his person because he had plenty of assistants to handle such details.

It is altogether possible in the near future that we will have a checkless, cashless society wherein each person would carry a master credit card that facilitates instant purchases, recording at the same time his or her address and relative shipping instructions. It's increasingly obvious that money is becoming ever more invisible—fewer of us are touching cash dollars fewer times in our day-to-day business transactions than ever before. Most people are paid by check, sometimes directly deposited into a bank account.

It would behoove you to wash and edit out the "money is dirty" idea from your mind. Neutralize that consciousness by affirming, "Money is wonderful stuff. It's clean and serves me perfectly. More will only serve me better."

2. "You don't know where it's been."

When I state this line, in seminars, it draws gales of laughter. Evidently, many parents have issued the indictment, "Don't put it in your mouth, you don't know where it's been." Money has regular resting places — banks, safes, wallets, pockets, purses and Prince Albert tobacco cans, but the innuendo is that these places and others are unsavory, unclean and probably germ-infested.

To a naive, evolving youngster who is a miniature experimental laboratory, test-tasting everything, money is no exception — whether its form is an asset called a baby crib or a diaper, coins or shells, or paper in Daddy's wallet.

Every child who spends time with Mom or Dad picks up on their thoughts and vibrations with regard to money. Money is the substance a child sees moving from one hand to another to obtain ice cream, candy and tickets to go on the rides at Disney World. It's the stuff that is exchanged for groceries every week at the market. It is even something that Mom and Dad fight about. Something so important as money is an emotionally charged subject. Many contradictory impressions fill the child's mind and may in fact be causing a money rejection complex for life.

My suggestion is to re-think and re-look at your feelings about money. Make sure those feelings are uniformly positive, because you *want* to manifest more money.

Anything this important deserves the attention of all five senses if at all possible. It's worth smelling, feeling, looking at, crinkling up or clicking together, listening to and, of course, tasting. Everything else goes into the open oral hatch, why not money?

3. "Don't put your hands in your mouth after you've handled money."

This is an extension of your parents telling you not to suck your thumb, it's unbecoming of a mature person. Americans in particular have a cleanliness fetish. We love things clean. The ambiance in the finest four-star restaurants, where waiters wear white gloves exemplifies this attitude.

Bank tellers who handle money all day long report that they wash their hands regularly before eating lunch and prior to leaving work. Dirt and green ink rub off on them and is deservedly washed away.

Without trying, a child watches money transformed into a myriad of other things. He or she thinks something along these lines: "It's just possible that by munching on that money, it will transform me into an adult. Then, instead of taking orders, I could give them. Instead of being imprisoned I could imprison. How utterly exciting and stimulating. If I get caught, who knows the consequences, besides I am adorable and lovable ... oh, oh, I can see that Mom doesn't like me eating dollar bills. Wow! Does she look mad! Stop! Stop! Stop spanking me! That hurts! I am innocent, I can't talk back or fight back. My only defense mechanism is real tears and loud crying. I'll quit and I'll never do it again. As a matter of fact, I've now got a deep-seated money rejection complex, the sting of which will stay bitterly with me for the rest of my life. It's invisible. It was imprinted during my emotional youth. I won't consciously be able to remember it, but that complex could turn me into a negligent bill payer and terrible creditor. Someday, maybe someone like Dr. Hansen will write about my innocent story and I'll see and intuitively remember the truth and be set free of the negative attitudes imposed in my childhood.

Affirm: "I like money and money likes me. I only do good with money and more money. My circulation of money enriches me and everyone else."

4. "All rich people are crooks."

The myth that rich people are crooks is inadvertently perpetrated by media and movies. These days, good guys rarely make it into TV-network prime time. The white-hatted businessperson is not generally considered newsworthy. "The Godfather" draws huge box-office receipts that no "How Good It Is" picture ever enjoyed. Rather, the negative and corrupt fraction of 1% of the business community continuously get the headlines and the feature stories. The author has had classes mark up the front page of any major metropolitan newspaper; they discover that 9 out of 10 cover stories are negative in nature. The individual reader is inundated with a mental overload of who's corrupt, cheating and involved in crime. The subconscious cannot take a joke. It does not discriminate. Whatever it is fed, it acts on and assumes to be true. Therefore, your subconscious becomes overwhelmed and assumes if the corrupt are getting all the attention and money with relatively few being caught, then it appears that crime pays and the really rich are corrupt.

It's not true. But the subconscious believes because, as Hitler's propagandists taught, whatever is repeated often enough becomes true to you. Scandals, robberies, embezzlement, thievery and other crimes crowd the news, while comparatively few powerfully positive business success stories hit the news. Possibly business people should band together to positively propagandize themselves and their success now.

To arrest the impact of all the negative and distorted media coverage, I recommend that you read only the Sunday Review section of the newspaper and/or a weekly news magazine like *Time* or *Newsweek*. It is imperative that you protect the input into your mind and believingly affirm before you ingest the news, "*I AM IMMUNE TO THIS NEGATIVE NEWS!*" Become habituated to saying this and you will feel better, stay happier, and be more pleasant because you'll be saying and affirming good things rather than, as one newspaper states, "All the *(BAD)* news fit to print."

Also, please do not watch the eleven o'clock news just prior to sleep. The subconscious never rests, and all night long it will be out robbing,

mugging, thugging, beating up and raping folks.
Instead, read your own *Future Diary*, your goal
sheets or something else positive, meaningful and
uplifting before you go to sleep.

To further neutralize the effect of news,
remember to invest the first 15 minutes of every
day reading some self-help action or inspirational
book.

5. "To get money and get ahead you've got to lie, steal, cheat and gamble."

Not true. The opposite is true, because the Law
of Mind is such that you get what you resist.
Therefore, if you lie to get ahead, the law of psychic
return insures that you will continually and
multiplyingly fear that others are lying to you and
about you. (For proof, investigate the deaths of
Judas Iscarot, Al Capone, Jimmy Hoffa and their
ilk.)

Worse yet, you won't be able to remember all
your past lies or how you covered them up. You'll
need bigger, more outrageous lies, and you'll
ultimately trap yourself in your own devious,
mischievious web because what goes around comes
around. Whatever you put out into the universe
comes back magnetized, magnified and multiplied
in your worry-filled mind. As Job said, "The thing I
have so greatly feared has come upon me."

Cheating always shows up sooner or later. To
the skillful at reading other people, it is witnessed in
700,000 subtle non-verbal communications.

The technology of catching cheaters is
becoming more sophisticated daily. There are
breath testers for assumed drunken drivers,
polygraphs for suspected criminals, voice detectors
which register fear and trepidation of heart in
seismic-like readings on the equivalent of a Richter
Scale, galvanic skin response sensors that can

monitor stress and read its most subtle fluctuation, aurometers read by psychics, and ever more monitoring equipment evolving. It should be noted that some individuals lie, cheat, steal and do other negative things in hopes of getting caught and capturing the media's attention, if only for a brief moment. One success philosopher said, "Everyone should be allowed to be famous at least once in a lifetime, for 15 minutes."

Gambling is a special case. It exists for the pleasure of those who pursue it as recreation in Las Vegas, Lake Tahoe, Reno, Atlantic City, the Bahama's and other places. Gambling is risk-taking with all the odds stacked in favor of the house. Most temporary winners get subtly addicted as they gamble, losing their normal restraints, inhibitions and common sense. Gambling is a lose-lose game. If you're going to do it, pre-establish the amount of money that you are willing to throw away. Then squander no more — stay disciplined. As you have a winning streak, immediately take half the proceeds and pocket them away so they are invisible to you. When you've won big, quit while you are ahead. If your luck takes a downturn, be smart: cut losses and quit early, fast and leave the gambling tables and casino.

Do not confuse gambling with business risk-taking. In business, smart people take calculated risks, which the really wise establish ahead of time. They promise themselves that if a deal goes sour they will not invest good money after bad — they'll kill the deal and create another. Insightful entrepreneurs are involved with their investments, but they possess their investments and do not let their investments possess them. The gambler's mindset is usually one that tends toward negative addiction, wherein the gambler becomes possessed by the game and then loses big. For example, newspaper and magazine stories have said that Sammy Davis Jr. lost so much money gambling that he had to sign a life long contract to work in Las Vegas to pay off his debt. Actor Walter Matthau is another compulsive gambler, who works to earn money to gamble, as he has stated in countless television interviews. The design of Las Vegas-like environments is slowly but surely to get you hooked on gambling.

6. "We can't afford this or that."

If you believe you can't afford something, the subconscious is cheerfully willing to help fulfill your belief. Jesus said, "It will be done unto you as you believe." Believe you can afford something and your subconscious will find ways you can which you may never have imagined.

Calvin Hunt, in Victoria, Texas, wrote in his *Future Diary* that he would purchase four $1000 tailor-made suits before the year's end. Suddenly it was December 28, and he had neither the money nor the suits. He attended an elegant party, and while there Calvin complimented a man on his superbly good-looking, excellently fitted suit. The man mentioned that he had had it tailor-made across the border in Mexico for $85 worth of labor with material costing $25 per yard. He was going to see his tailor the next day, the man said, and invited Calvin along for a fitting. As a result, Calvin purchased four $1,000 suits for a total of $1,000, and he had them by the end of the year. His dream came true because he wrote it down on paper and in his mind believed, expected the dream to happen somehow and finally took action.

Obviously, whether you believe you can afford something or not, you're right.

The appropriate attitude to take is this: *Make*

your decision to afford whatever first, then find the money.
The cliche I wrote says, "You make the decision and
the subconscious makes the provision." When you
ask the infinite intelligence within you to discover a
certain amount of money by a certain time for a
certain purpose that you are emotionally excited
about, it will generally fulfill your wish. Especially if
you have a track record of similar successful
accomplishments — that's when you can take
quantum leaps forward. My mail abounds with
letters from people who came to believe they could
do extraordinary things and did.

Be careful to remember the real source of *all*
good is God. There are an infinite number of
potential delivery channels to meet your every need
when you are open, positive and receptive to your
own greater good.

Dr. Robert Schuller, founder and senior pastor
of the Crystal Cathedral, was just that. For almost
20 years he kept building bigger and bigger projects
involving and evolving continually greater sums of
money until he had the penultimate of cathedral
ideas: the magnificent Crystal Cathedral, in
Garden Grove, California. Originally, he estimated
its costs at $6 million, and he made a decision to ask
for that money. His possible solutions were that he
could find: 1) one person to give $6 million for the
cathedral; 2) six people to give $1 million each (he
ultimately found seven million-dollar donors,
including Frank Sinatra and John Wayne); or 3)
12,000 individuals, each of whom would purchase a
window with his or her name on it for $500. He
accomplished this final fund-raising option twice
over, the second time selling little stars to hang
proudly in the glass super-structure that is the
largest such edifice in the world. His costs, due to
design, size and earthquake considerations,
exceeded $18 million. The Crystal Cathedral is a

must to visit and see. It exemplifies the belief that a man or woman with a great idea, big desire and tremendous amounts of active drive can do anything.

God's riches are inexhaustible. The world is rich. You are in the world and you deserve to be rich. It is you birthright—all you have to do is imagine your riches and work to build a foundation under your vital, vibrant ideas. Whether you have a high aim or a low aim, you will hit it. No aim is a low aim. So have high aims.

You can afford anything you *really want*. No goal is unrealistic, only your time frame to accomplish it may be too short. Also, you may need the support and cooperative harmony of what Napoleon Hill, in his excellent book, *Think and Grow Rich*, calls a "Master Mind Alliance," a union of individuals who want to help you accomplish whatever you want to do by using their skills in alliance to your aims. Several individuals dedicated to working together in the spirit of cooperative harmony form a new, more powerful mind. The idea of cooperative harmony is best pictured by putting two straight index fingers together — do you see the number eleven? The effect is synergetic in nature, which means that the behavior of the whole system cannot be predicted from that of the individual parts. Individuals working in concerted, well-orchestrated harmony are incredibly powerful. Gather around yourself supportive allies who want what you want. The result will astound and gratify you.

7. "Money doesn't buy happiness."

It's true that money doesn't necessarily buy happiness, but then neither does its counterpart, poverty.

Money exists in utter abundance for those who

will perform a service to obtain her. (Money is generically female, with a personality that wants to be romanced to be obtained.)

John Paul Getty once said there are enough "needs" available to facilitate everyone in the world becoming a millionaire, That's true.

It's also true that what bankers call the velocity of money, or how fast money moves or rolls over in the economy, is ever increasing. The velocity of money increased from one annual use of a gold or silver coin per person to literally thousands of annual roll-overs thanks to checks, credit cards, and computerized banking. For paper money, the Federal Reserve reports that the average lean-green dollar bill's life expectancy in the 1980's is only one and one half years and that every American alive has approximately $500 cash to use annually.

What does all this have to do with happiness? Lots! It means: a) money is available; b) it's yours for rendering a higher quantity of higher quality service with a positive mental attitude; and c) positive self-image psychologists have determined that a large percentage of one's self-worth is often created best in what is called work. Therefore, the old work ethic does have redeeming virtues. Especially when the worker is gainfully involved in a pursuit that makes him or her satisfied and fulfilled while he or she is serving greatly and providing real benefits. Remember, every human being is needed. Every one of us has talent and should continually attempt to maximize himself or herself. Peter Drucker, the premier American management guru and theoretician, says once every seven years—exactly how often the human body totally regenerates itself—individuals should recycle themselves into a new occupation or totally change the way they do what they do. In a similar vein, the late Walt Disney, as he created EPCOT City (the Experimental Prototipical City Of Tomorrow, in Orlando, Florida) for company retirees, dedicated his project to retired workers. He said, "No retiree can live here unless he or she is working."

The life insurance industry's actuarial statistics prove that if you retire from something to nothing, you expire within a year. Metaphysically and spiritually speaking, this happens because the mind is a teleologically- or ends-oriented mechanism that must always be fulfilling some objective. That's why I wrote *Future Diary*, so readers would participate to write out all their goals, hopes, dreams, desires, high aspirations and high ideals to teach themselves to be happy and stay in the continual pursuit of goal setting and goal getting.

It is imperative that every individual have too many goals rather than too few. Goals are a preview of future events, literally magnetizing you to your own greater good. Create goals that are positive, purposeful and life-benefiting, otherwise, your teleologically-oriented mind will automatically self-destruct, disintegrate, and self-annihilate.

I know, because my mother did. She had only two great goals in life. One was to make sure my dad, my brothers and I were happy and healthy. She accomplished this objective in a sublime way. She inundated each of us with love and more love. She was an idyllic mama who deserved to be placed on a pedestal. She overflowed with abundant, heartfelt generosity, enthusiasm and smiles, constantly claiming, "I have the best boys on the block." We appreciated her love, praise, support, encouragement and adulation, and we became the best boys on the block.

Her second goal was to see us through college. My little brother went to school so long that when people asked my dad, "What will your son be when he graduates?" my dad said, "29." When my brother did graduate from college, with honors, my mom's goals and role in life were over. She had nothing new to live for. She became an alcoholic, dying from a five-finger liver. It was painful to watch her self-destruct because she lacked love and its intrinsic goals. That's why I say, "Have too many goals, not too few," because all goals will soon enough be realized.

The Bible says, "Love your neighbor as yourself." That means you have to have positive and correct self-love first. When my mom's goals and roles were accomplished she was left feeling useless, without direction, unloved and unworthy, because at some levels she saw herself as unneeded and unloved. She somehow believed that her expression of love was meant to be only that of totally facilitating my brothers' and my growth into adulthood. Then her flame's brightness and utility was to flicker and fade away. She chose to have a bout with booze. Unfortunately, like the majority of self-annihilating alcoholics, she lost. She died in her sleep. This process is humiliating, painful and ugly to watch. One in 10 Americans is an alcoholic because he or she lacks the goal of sobriety.

Every alcoholic affects 25 people directly and indirectly: family members, friends and those in one's energy orbit. I was young and impressionable and I grieved as I witnessed my mother's self-degeneration. I lost energy, ate too much and spent excessive hours sleeping. I wanted to help. Doesn't every concerned, caring friend and relative want to help, all of whom are considered meddlers by the alcoholic? I took my mom to a rehabilitation center to dry out. When I did, amongst her last, lashing words to me were, "I hate you." That hurt. She didn't really mean it. What she actually was crying out was, "I don't love me — how can you?"

My experience described above has many mini-lessons:

1) Love yourself first, positively and correctly, for then and only then can you love others and be happy.

2) Create for yourself what you really want. Daily cocktails and regular social drinking guarantees alcoholism, and that doesn't make anyone I know happy, especially over a long period of time.

3) Money has great benefits for you and others. Beneficial uses of money will make you truly happy. With surplus money in excess of your every personal, family and corporate need, you can philanthropically create libraries like Andrew Carnegie did; art museums like Norton Simon and J. Paul Getty did; living museums like William Randolph Hearst and George Vanderbilt did; parks; hospitals; or space, sea and mind exploration projects, all of which desperately need your mental and financial power.

8. "Rich people are unhappy."

That's a myth propagated by the poor to justify their own lack of initiative and industry.

Rich or poor individuals are about as happy as they choose to be.

Happiness is a by-product of doing, being, having and thinking something. It is not really an end goal.

Gurus counsel: "Be happy," and such affirmation helps to stimulate you to think happy thoughts, take happy actions and accomplish results that will make you happy.

Bob Hope is very rich, as stated elsewhere, probably close to a billionaire who holds with real estates, oil and other investments. Yet anyone can see he is happy while being totally productive and philanthropic.

Similar examples abound in their availability. Remember, we learn by imitation, identification, instruction and example. Choose good role models to imitate and identify with in your ascent to become very rich.

Many rich people are very happy. Liberace says, "You tell the men from the boys by the price of their toys." For a really enjoyable experience read Liberace's autobiography, *The Things I Love*. It is written in his opulent and affluent style, with beautiful and inspiring pictures of him. He has totally thought out his belief system and it's exciting reading. When he read Claude Bristol's paperback self-help book, *The Magic of Believing*, he bought into the belief, "You can believe and do anything you really want to." He wanted to and has made classical music available to the masses. He says, "I did not want to be Paderewski." I interviewed him once in a Las Vegas jewelry store and asked if he had done everything he ever wanted to do. He answered, "Yes, 'til now, but I have a lot more wants."

Liberace is a masterful performer. If possible, catch his act, read his books and visit his Las Vegas-based museum. His outrageous museum stimulates one's ideation to extravagance. The entry-fee proceeds go toward sholarships to further aspiring young musicians. Liberace's museum and self-perpetuating scholarship fund are good examples of his dreams come true.

Again, this exemplifies win-win-win behavior,

where everyone is better off and no one is worse off. Everyone wants to view celebrities, environments and accouterments. Liberace has been generous and has opened his windows so anyone interested can look in and vicariously enjoy the treat.

9. "I am on welfare."

Well, get off! There is no free lunch, and welfare robs you of your self-esteem, self-respect and self-reliance. My friend Rev. Ike, the money-minister, is the only minister I know who shows stacks of letters from people he has personally inspired through his preaching, teaching, tapes and literature to get out of the welfare line and back into the work line. This is the kind of effort that should be heralded by media. He teaches positive self-image psychology and raises individuals' self-esteem, encouraging them to use their mind-power to obtain all the green power they would like. He is so extraordinary that I recommend a special trip to New York City to take in his uptown Broadway show every Sunday at 3:00 p.m. at the United Palace. It will excite the good-spell (God-spell) in you.

Another similar example of "off the welfare lines" was shared with me in a lecture by Dr. Eric Butterworth of New York City. Dr. Butterworth explained that a two-week workshop was given to the hard-core unemployed "welfare-victims" in positive self-image psychology, replete with daily experiences in visualization, verbalization, imagination and future realization studies. At the end of two intensive weeks of study, 95% of the attendees obtained work. Two years later, a follow-up study conducted by the welfare department discovered 98% of those inaugurally employed were still employed. Due to vested, myopic interests, the welfare department classified the report. As you know, the Washington-based welfare lobbyists have the biggest lobby in D.C., one a hundred times bigger financially than its next closest competitor. It's a crime. Instead, our educational system could and should be teaching positive self-image psychology. I, and other motivators I know, would cheerfully welcome welfare people into our seminars, free. If they attended in small numbers and gained a feeling of self-respect, rekindled their enthusiasms, I feel sure they would seek and find gainful employment. There must be a way to do it — perhaps you will conceive it.

It is important to note that demonstrating prosperity is more important than teaching about it. A poor person cannot show another poor person how to get rich. However, every rich person I've mentioned has written books, given interviews and shared greatly to stimulate ever more prosperity.

In this vein I would like to encourage you totally to visit the following places. Each takes an investment of one-half to a full day to relish the full experience. Each offers tour guides and books to help you really grasp the vital insights of prosperity. After visiting 10 or more of these places, I am sure you will know that most of the rich are happy on many levels. (Please send this author new names and other ideas to be added to this list for future editions of this book.)

1. Liberace's Museum, Las Vegas, Nevada

2. The Hearst Castle, San Simeon, California

3. The Getty Mansion, Malibu, California

4. The Huntington Library and Art Gallery, Pasadena, California

5. The Biltmore Estate, Ashville, North Carolina (seen in the movie "Being There" with

Peter Sellers)

6. President Theodore Roosevelt's home, Sagamore Hill, Long Island, New York

7. President Franklin and Eleanor Roosevelt's home, Hyde Park, New York

8. Viscaya, The John Deer Museum, Miami, Florida

9. Thomas Alva Edison's home and laboratory, Ft. Myers, Florida

10. Tours of the stars' homes, Beverly Hills, California

11. Tours of the stars' homes, Palm Springs, California

12. New York City tour of Manhattan (this place is loaded with exciting places to follow up)

13. United Palace, Rev. Ike's opulent church at 175th and Broadway, New York, New York

14. Winchester House, San Jose, California

15. Rich neighborhoods everywhere you go for inspiration

16. Guided tours everywhere you go. They are fascinating, entertaining and informative.

10. "Christ was a poor carpenter."

This is a myth propagandized during the Dark Ages to further enslave the masses to bondage to the church and political state, which were then inexorably intertwined.

Dr. Catherine Ponder's excellent book, *The Millionaire From Nazareth*, published by DeVorss in Santa Monica, California, truly reveals that Christ always thought, worked, acted and taught prosperity. He said, "I am here that you might have the abundant life." and, "Seek ye first the Kingdom (inner realization) and *allllll* things (fine clothes, fine cars, fine homes, fine jewelry, great friends, love, peace and harmony) shall be added unto you."

Christ converted a lack of fishes into lots of fishes, leaving 12 baskets left over, teaching us the first laws of conservation.

When the tax collector in Capernaum asked to be paid, Christ didn't say, "I am from Nazareth." Rather, he said, "Peter, go and cast a line in the lake; take the first fish that comes to the hook, open it's mouth, and you will find a silver coin;take that and pay it in; it will meet the tax for us both."

Christ always lived from abundance. It's all he knew. In truth, that's all there is — abundance, but "many have eyes and cannot see" (riches, affluence, opulence and every good thing awaiting the insight of your invisible, inner eye). Look at nature for the truth of abundance. Think about one sunflower seed growing into a plant of 10,000 sunflower seeds by harvest time.

God created the world to be regeneratively abundant. Christ knew, understood and taught the same, saying always, "Go thou and do likewise." This means there is more than enough. As the singing Psalmist, David, said, "My cup runneth over." Yours does too, when you understand that God — infinite wisdom, infinite love and total awareness — knew, "like birds of the field, you'd have need of these things and like lilies of the field, who toil not but always have enough." That doesn't mean you should live on welfare, an inheritance or a hand-out. It means you have a divine right and obligation to work, be productive daily, and provide yourself with any good thing you desire.

Remember that Christ only got uptight once in the four gospels, when he said to the servant who buried his talent, "Oh, you wicked and slothful servant." You and I are meant to maximize and fully employ our talents, gifts and abilities. It's not okay to be lazy — mentally, physically, socially or spiritually. Only you can continually outperform, outproduce and outgrow your yesterday's best. Congratulations.